TRANSPORTING YOUR HORSE
OR PONY

TRANSPORTING YOUR HORSE OR PONY

Chris Larter and Tony Jackson

DAVID & CHARLES
Newton Abbot London North Pomfret (Vt)

British Library Cataloguing in Publication Data
Larter, Chris
  Transporting your horse or pony.
  1. Horses – Transportation
  I. Title II. Jackson, Tony, *1937–*
  636.1'083   SF285

  ISBN 0–7153–8938–X

Photographs by Tony Jackson,
Chris Larter and Sharon Cregier

Line illustrations by Joy Claxton

Phototypeset in Linotron Trump Mediaeval
by Northern Phototypesetting Co, Bolton
and printed in Great Britain
by Redwood Burn Limited, Trowbridge
for David & Charles Publishers plc
Brunel House Newton Abbot Devon

Published in the United States of America
by David & Charles Inc
North Pomfret Vermont 05053 USA

Contents

Foreword

When I was asked to write a short foreword to Chris Larter's latest book my first reaction was that there was no one better than Chris to write a book about transporting horses.

I first met Chris in the late Sixties when I started to travel abroad. Chris had already been on the circuit for a few years then. In those days she was travelling horses for Ann Moore who, in the early Seventies, was hugely successful and travelled a great deal. On those lengthy trips across Europe with all the inevitable hold-ups at borders and long nights on cross-Channel ferries, Chris was always the one to raise the morale of the whole party with her bubbling personality and endless humorous stories of her life in the horse world.

More than all that she obviously possesses not only a great affection for her horses, but a deep understanding of their well-being and comfort. I have always felt that it is not the jumping itself which shortens a horse's career but getting to the show and back again. Make no mistake, travelling is very wearing on a horse. It cannot tell you if it is not feeling well or is dog-tired and the Chris Larters of the horse world have to possess a sixth sense to assess not only when a horse gets sick, but before it happens.

There is no substitute for job experience and Chris has that in plenty. Having moved on from travelling show-jumpers, she then set up her own horse-transporting business and is always in great demand by well-known owners and competitors to ferry their horses around – that is a great commendation in itself. Show-jumpers, including myself, are very particular who handles their horses and she would not have lasted so long in her profession without the ability and knowledge to keep both horses and their owners happy. I hope this book enjoys the success which Chris Larter so richly deserves.

STEPHEN HADLEY
KINETON, WARWICKSHIRE

Preface

Although a few of the equestrian magazines have, from time to time, published articles on horse and pony transport, this is, I believe, the first book designed to cover every aspect of this vital subject. The idea was first suggested to me by the former Editor of *Shooting Times* magazine, Tony Jackson, an old friend who lives in my area and has been involved with horses and the hunting scene for many years.

A great deal of my life has been involved with the professional transportation of horses and ponies, both in this country and abroad and, naturally, I have gained a wealth of knowledge and tips from my mistakes and experiences. All this has been assembled in the hope that many people will be helped and some unnecessary accidents avoided. There are many unforeseen dangers lurking in the horse world, some where you would least expect them, and many before you even get on the road. So often all that is required is a little thought and common sense and I have given several examples to illustrate the dangers which can assail the unwary. You cannot be too careful with horses.

This book is intended for the amateur horse or pony owner who wants to 'go it alone'. The best of luck!

CHRIS LARTER

Chapter 1

Trailer or Horsebox?

1

Until the 1920s travelling a horse entailed hiring a box to go by rail or, quite simply, getting on the animal's back. Hacking on to a meet, or sending your groom ahead with the horses, perhaps the day before if the meet was a fair distance, to stop overnight, was the normal practice. However, by the 1870s and '80s it was quite the done thing to take your horse by train, special boxes being attached to the carriages.

In those days, if the facility of the railway was not available, or you lacked the benefit of a groom, you simply rode to the meet, hunted and rode home. Distances covered were, in today's terms, colossal. A 15–20 mile (24–32km) hack to meet hounds and a day's hunting and then home might tally anything up to 50–60 miles (80–96km) for the day. Little wonder that riders and horses were really hard and fit in those distant days.

However, by the 1930s boxes and trailers were readily available and greatly in demand. The Hammond-Newmarket Horsebox, for instance, a splendid self-contained unit, with side ramp, could be acquired for £395; Vincents of Reading could produce a two-horse box model on a 6-cylinder chassis for a similar amount, while the Lambourn Luxury Patent Horse-Box in which, we are told, horses and attendants travelled first-class, could be built according to customer's requirements – and priced accordingly.

Today, anyone owning a horse or pony will require, sooner or later, to transport the animal some distance, perhaps to a local show, to ride with friends, to take it to an area which has better hacking country or to hunt. Borrowing a trailer or horsebox is by no means always convenient and there is always the danger of an accident or possible damage which can be embarrassing. Hiring, on a regular basis, can prove extremely expensive and is really impractical if one intends to participate on a consistent basis in events which demand transporting the animal.

For the complete beginner the most important initial question is that of choice. Should one decide upon a trailer or go for a motorised vehicle? Not unnaturally the first consideration must usually be the price. By virtue of the fact that it is a self-contained unit, a horsebox usually tends to be expensive. Most novices initially prefer to choose a trailer.

However, before a decision can be made there are many aspects which must be considered. Let's look first at trailers.

The first thing to appreciate is that it is not simply a question of buying a trailer and bolting a tow-bar to your car. You must take into consideration the size of the horse or pony, and, of course, there may be more than one. Is your car sufficiently large and powerful enough to pull, as a minimum, two ponies in a lightweight trailer? Certainly, you could get away with no less than a 1,600cc car, while for two big horses 2 litres is the bare minimum. Even then, there is likely to be excessive wear on the gearbox. The first essential is to check with your dealer or friendly garage to ascertain the car's maximum towing weight. The information should be contained in the vehicle's documents, but it is wise to have it confirmed.

The ideal vehicle, if you are towing a trailer (and if you can afford it) is a Range Rover, or at least a Land-Rover or heavy four-wheel drive. If you take your animal to shows or have to park your trailer on verges you will soon come to appreciate the benefit of four-wheel drive. One of the most common sights at horse shows is trailers towed by cars being in turn pulled out of greasy or muddy ground by tractors.

The actual choice of trailer can depend on whether you require a lightweight or a heavier model. One particular trailer on the market today has proved very popular because of its aerodynamic design. Not only is it lighter and easier to tow but it can produce fuel savings of up to 20 per cent.

If you have only one animal and decide on a single rather than a double trailer, then do make certain you purchase a 'broad' single rather than a narrow one, unless you are perhaps only intending to transport a tiny pony or perhaps a donkey. I cannot imagine how any thinking owner can dare to travel a reasonably sized pony or horse in a narrow trailer. The animal can easily panic from claustrophobia and turn the vehicle over. One has only to travel behind a single trailer to realise just how dangerous they can be.

If, however, you choose to go to the other extreme and acquire a three-horse trailer, do appreciate that you will require a heavy, powerful vehicle to pull it, especially if it is ever fully loaded.

Some animals intensely dislike travelling in a trailer. On numerous occasions I have had telephone calls from worried and anxious owners who believe that their horse or pony is nervous in a trailer and would be happier and less restive in a box. The reason for the upset is often claustrophobia, stemming from the fact that the animal has suffered from a bad ride, despite the owner's honest belief that he or she has driven carefully. Inevitably, there must be a certain amount of sway in the trailer, which does little to encourage the animal once it has suffered a bad fright. It may take a great deal of time and patience to overcome its fear and some animals never recover. For these it is far safer to travel them in a box. It may be expensive but it is far better than to risk a sad and distressing disaster.

Today, new trailers can vary in price from about £800 to £2,500, but if this range is beyond your pocket it is usually possible to pick up a suitable second-hand one. However, as with anything which is not new there are snags and pitfalls set to trap the unwary. Second-hand trailers can be bought privately (often the best recourse) through dealers or at auction. If you know a reliable dealer or have had one recommended he will probably sell you a good, honest trailer but naturally you will have to pay rather more than in a private deal.

But by whatever method you choose to buy, one of the first and most important areas to check is the floor. If this shows the slightest signs of being unsafe, exhibiting traces of rot in the corners or lifting boards, don't buy it unless you are prepared to put in a new floor, preferably with double hardwood. Corners of trailers are particularly susceptible to

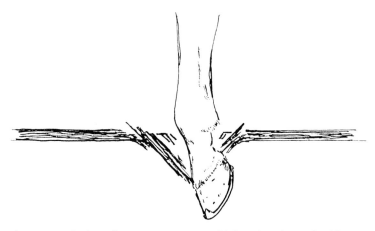

A rotten timber floor can prove a frightening hazard. Always carefully check the floors of secondhand trailers

wood-rot as straw tends to pile up unless it is cleaned out scrupulously. Any dampness underneath (some folk have a tendency to use their trailers as travelling latrines) soon eats away at the boarding. The dreadful stories one hears of horses crashing through the floor while the vehicle is moving are, sadly, all too true – an unbearable thought.

Most older trailers have wooden floors, but these are rapidly being replaced by new designs with floors being surfaced in tough substances such as granilastic or cork. Personally, I am not keen on the use of rubber-mats on a wooden floor because when the trailer is washed out, as it should be every time it is used, the water can all too easily become trapped underneath the rubber and, as it will never dry out, quickly rots the wood. Manure also has the same effect, working its way around the edges of the mats and underneath them.

In the majority of trailers it is usual for the horses to travel facing forwards, so it is essential to have a well-padded breast-bar in front of them to prevent them from hitting their heads on the front of the trailer in the event of a sudden stop. I much prefer a breast-bar for each horse, rather than a long one for two animals as the latter can create problems when trying to take out just one animal forwards because you may find two trying to get out at once.

Breast-bars should be fixed so that, while they can be quickly undone by the groom, the horse itself cannot release them. Bars and pins must be really tough as they can sometimes be called upon to sustain a great deal of weight if you should have to brake suddenly in an emergency. It has even been known for some horses to 'climb' the breast-bars, getting themselves into an awkward situation, for if they become wedged it is almost impossible to extricate them without assistance. I have on two occasions seen this happen

Keep an eye on the ramp springs. Never remove one when the ramp is down

at shows when the trailer was standing still.

Breeching straps behind the animals are essential. They should be constructed of a very tough and unyielding material in case the horse tries to sit back on them when the ramp is lowered, or it attempts to shoot out backwards after it has been loaded. If chains are used, they should be covered, but I dislike them because, sooner or later, the cover splits and, should the horse suddenly pull back, your fingers can all too easily be trapped. Never overlook, or be careless about, broken breech straps. A man was fatally injured while attempting to raise a ramp behind two horses, neither of which had a breech strap behind it. They panicked and backed out at the crucial moment, crushing the man beneath the ramp.

Look after your ramp springs, too, because even trailer ramps, which are comparatively much smaller than lorry ramps, can be surprisingly heavy, particularly if they are reinforced and have thick hessian or rubber matting on them.

A commercial horsebox showing the back section of stalls for horses facing forwards

A large commercial box with two side ramps and back ramp

If a spring should snap, replace it at once or, far the better course, invest in a new pair, as it is probably an indication that the other spring is also nearing the end of its life. I hope you are not in the firing line if a spring does break as it can go off like a jack-in-the-box!

My own preference is for a trailer with a front-unloading ramp. I always think that if a horse has to back out it is encouraging it to do so when not required, and a rear unload sometimes makes the horse more difficult to load, especially if it is difficult to start with. If on the other hand, it can see where it is going, it is less inclined to panic.

A few years ago there was considerable discussion on the merits or otherwise of travelling horses backwards in trailers. One particular trailer, the Kiwi Safety Trailer, was pronounced ideal. The loading method, however, involved raising the ramp to create a platform about 14in (36cm) above the ground, leading the horse up on to it, and then backing it in to the trailer. One was assured that, after a little training,

A polo artic showing herring-bone sideways partitions

most horses would quickly adapt to the method.

Certainly, it might have been ideal if you had only your own horse to deal with, but of little advantage if you were asked, for instance, to give a lift to someone else's horse. It was considered that to overcome this objection the horse should enter at the front of the trailer, when it would walk in forwards and face the rear. However, it seemed that design problems prohibited most trailer companies from adapting a front-unload trailer to front loading. Yet, from a handler's point of view, it would seem much easier to use this method, rather than have to encourage the horse on to a raised platform, turn it round and then back it in to the trailer, particularly so if two horses were involved.

Yet if horses were loaded from the front to face the rear, the trailer would probably be heavier at the forward end and thus exert extra wear on the towing vehicle's engine, quite apart from increased fuel consumption, and in addition, the ramp would add extra weight.

Nevertheless, it was generally agreed that horses did, in fact, travel well facing the rear and were able to balance themselves perfectly and also brace themselves against breaking and deceleration. However, commercial considerations had to be taken into account and it was concluded that the capital expenditure and investment would be too great, while manufacturers would have to come up with a fresh range of designs and towing vehicles.

Dr Sharon Cregier of Canada has argued that a single entry/ exit rear-face trailer would require no additional expenditure by the manufacturer when on the assembly line. She claims that no more than a single placement change of axle and tow-bar adjustment would be required. In fact, rear-facing travel offers considerably increased scope to designers to produce a low-profile aerodynamic bulkhead over the horse's rump to help save on fuel. This, however, will not happen overnight. The Kiwi trailer is no longer made, but a rear-face trailer is manufactured by a Blackpool firm. Only a regular demand would ensure that rear-face trailers would replace conventional ones and this seems unlikely at the moment.

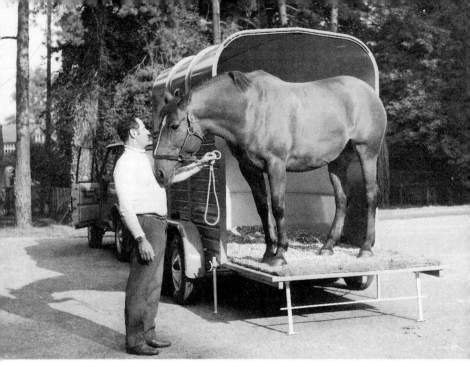

The Kiwi trailer: the horse has been led up on to the platform, a manoeuvre whith which very few horses have problems

The horse's quarters have been moved round, and he has been backed into the trailer. To unload, the platform's stabilising legs are folded down so that, when lowered, it forms a conventional ramp down which the horse can walk forwards

It may well be that, given a choice, horses prefer to travel facing backwards. I have occasionally towed a trailer carrying a mare and foal and have usually removed the partition and placed a grid in the space over the ramp as horses travelled loose have been known to scramble out of this gap, incredible though it may seem. In the case of mares and foals, however, they have usually proved no trouble and the mare would always turn round to face the rear if not tied up. However, you need to drive with extreme caution because if the mare turns while you are moving she can easily unbalance the trailer. You may prefer to tie the mare up.

It always amazes me to learn how many people totally ignore the basic safety rules of trailers. Possibly because the trailer is itself not motorised, they assume that there is little that can require attention. However, it is surprising just how many parts on a trailer need constant checking and attention.

Make sure, for a start, that the brake linkage is adjusted and lubricate the moving linkage; examine the wheel-bearings, packing in grease twice a year and constantly examine the tyres for bulges, cracks, nails, worn tread and pressure. Soft or unequal pressures will increase the drag on the towing vehicle, inflate fuel consumption and may well make the trailer unstable. Always carry a spare wheel and make certain that all wheels and hub-caps are secure. I find it virtually impossible to shift nuts that have been blown on with a pressure pump and much prefer that they should be hand tightened. Needless to say, you must have a jack and a tyre wrench.

Check that all your lights and indicators are working, giving between 60 and 120 flashes per minute when plugged into the trailer. It is vital that all electrical connections are kept clean and sound. The answer is always to keep them covered, perhaps with a plastic cover, when the trailer is not in use.

When you are considering a second-hand trailer, check for broken weld spots, leaks, loosened covering or lining and blocked ventilators. Make sure there are no splinters inside the trailer, or sharp metal protrusions or loose screws on

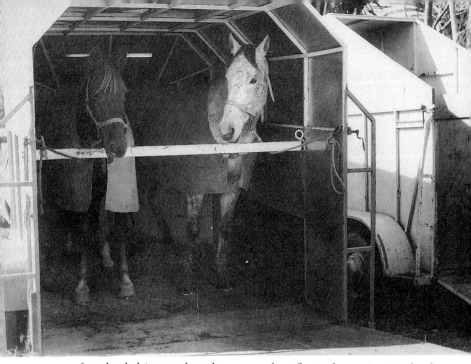

Just loaded into a three-horse rear-face float, these New Zealand show-jumpers assume the relaxed position that they maintain in transit. Note the unmarked interior of the float compared to the adjacent forward-facing trailer. The tying method shown is not recommended

which a horse can damage itself. As I have already mentioned, wet manure on the trailer floor can be deadly if it is left, so check the boarding carefully for worn, rotten or slippery patches. If the wood is getting soft, don't hesitate to replace it with hardwood or plywood treated with a suitable preservative.

Keep all the bolts greased, particularly on the partitions, as there is nothing more annoying than being unable to move a partition when you want to because the bolts have rusted into their slots. Likewise, oil the locks on the breeching straps so that they can be fastened and released easily. The same applies to the ramp lugs.

The tow-bar is a vital element so make certain that there is a good quality one on the trailer and have a 50mm tow-ball fitted to your towing vehicle. There are, unfortunately, a few sub-standard tow-balls of between 48mm and 52mm on the market which, if fitted, could cause the trailer coupling to lift off the ball while in transit and cause an accident. Never be tempted to file a tow-ball to make it fit. All tow-balls and couplings will become worn with use and should be checked regularly. In the case of an accident, however slight, inspect the tow-ball and tow-bar for any damage and don't hesitate to replace them if you are in doubt.

Good quality trailers are extremely popular with thieves so it is wise to invest in a lock and, of course, make certain that the unit is insured.

If, on the other hand, you decide that you prefer a horsebox, remember that many of the rules mentioned above will still apply.

You will not be able to purchase the ideal box; such a

This prototype of a front entry, rear exit, walk-through float has since been modified. Windows behind the travelling horses are not recommended

A horse and pony loaded into the rear-face New Zealand float. At no time is the handler in the kicking zone of the horse

vehicle has not been made simply because everyone has their own ideas and what suits one person may not suit another.

One of the first considerations is size. Will you require living quarters in the box? Or will it be simply used to transport horses and equipment without this luxury? The price will vary enormously depending on your requirement as living quarters add enormously to the cost.

Today, there is a wide range of designs and materials, used both inside and outside the vehicle. Which way, for instance, do you want the horses to face? Do you prefer to have them travelling facing forwards or diagonally across? In some horseboxes two face forwards and two backwards and although they are all loaded by the side ramp, the horses at the rear are unloaded down the back ramp. A lorry which carries horses across need only have a back ramp, thus lessening the weight factor.

Ramps are a vital part of any horse-conveyance system, whether it is a box or a trailer, yet are frequently neglected. They take a great deal of wear and tear and constantly need maintenance. Bare boards quickly become slippery and give no grip to a horse, so they must have some form of covering. I prefer rubber set between the lats because, although heavier than coconut matting, unlike the latter it does not wear.

As with trailers, keep an eye on your ramp springs and never, under any circumstances, attempt to remove one when the ramp is down. Some years ago a well-known show-jumper was hit in the face by a spring, causing serious injuries and on another occasion a young lady went to let a ramp down, unaware that during the night thieves had stolen the ramp springs. The heavy ramp fell and crushed her, leaving her paralysed.

One of the major problems with boxes is the sheer weight of the ramp. I have driven many horseboxes but have found very few ramps which I can lift comfortably on my own. I am sure that this is something to which manufacturers should apply themselves. The ideal is, of course, a push-button automatic ramp, but these are expensive and can on occasion fail. A problem with wooden ramps is that they can sometimes swell when they become very wet, the result being that they jam and are very difficult to open and close.

There are several types of ramp fasteners on the market. The ones which I particularly dislike are those which wind in from either side for they can work loose, and one need hardly emphasise the danger if a ramp falls while the vehicle is in motion. This has happened to me twice; fortunately, on neither occasion was any harm done, but I know one case in which a child was killed when a ramp fell on a pavement.

Make absolutely sure that the floor is sufficiently strong. This applies, in particular, to converted furniture vans. I recall once borrowing a lorry which, I discovered to my horror, had been left for months with rotting manure on the floor. When I mucked it out I was able to sink my fork 1½in (38mm) into the wood. Needless to say, I did not use it.

If you are considering converting a van, remember that the

There are very few ramps on boxes which lift comfortably

walls will require strengthening and lining, and don't forget the vents. Containers already built to carry horses will naturally have all this, although some have small vents in the roof which are not suitable because they let in rainwater and are often inaccessible when horses are loaded. Horses require fresh air, but beware of direct draughts in cold weather. This is the time to rug up as well, especially if the horses are clipped out.

If I have any grey hairs they have been caused by partitions. They are the most awkward, contrary and difficult objects I have had to deal with. While they need to be both tough and strong, at the same time, by virtue of these qualities, they are heavy, clumsy and seldom fit squarely. Many have appallingly stiff spring-bolts which are supposed to fit into holes in the floor and ceiling but seldom line up. They are meant to be foolproof but I have on several occasions known the bolts in a partition to jump from the sockets, causing the entire contraption to crash on the unfortunate horse. Many times I have cursed the person who invented them, for I guarantee that if you do not already have a bad back, ill-fitting spring-bolts will rapidly provide you with one, and if you do, they'll make it worse. Most transport drivers who use them regularly dislike them but nothing seems to be done about the problem. Sometimes they can be downright dangerous. I once had a spring-bolt snap and shoot out of its 'pocket', causing the partition to swing out of the side of the horsebox. It came down heavily on my arm, bruising it badly.

Be careful not to get your toes or fingers trapped by spring-bolts and it is important to keep them well greased despite the mess you will get on your hands. Either wear a pair of old gloves or keep some wet-wipes and paper rolls handy in the cab. Personally, I much prefer pins to fasten partitions, but they must be horseproof.

In a box, if your horses face forwards they will need to have a breast-bar or a door in front of them, not just a blank wall. If you brake suddenly, or have a collision, an animal could get a split head or broken neck unless there is something against its chest to absorb the shock. This has happened, so be warned.

Two horses in an area intended for three to allow extra room on a long journey; Kings Troop RHA horses en route to Berlin Tatoo

Make sure, too, that your horse has plenty of room. Cramped quarters will only encourage him to lean or 'scrabble' with his feet when you drive round bends and if he does fall he will have insufficient room to get up. On the other hand, if he has a wide stall he will learn to balance himself by spreading his legs just as you would in a moving train.

A horse does not necessarily have to stand like a grazing giraffe to keep his balance, particularly if he has something to help him grip the floor. Some modern flooring has a certain amount of grip but I always like to put down a little bedding, preferably shavings which also soak up the wet and help reduce any smell. I dislike rubber mats or coconut matting as both tend to become scraped up underneath the horse, while they are also heavy, messy and smelly. One advantage of modern flooring, including that with a fixed rubber overlay, is that it can be hosed out easily. If you have living quarters you will need a ledge between them and the floor so that the water does not slop into them.

Living quarters are an absolute boon if you intend to spend a considerable time at shows. To be able to make cups of tea between classes, and to have somewhere to sit in comfort, especially on cold days is a great advantage. There is a wide range of designs available, most of which are very practical, and if you are having a horsebox built or converted, you can design quarters to suit your requirements. While, as I have said, most designs are practical, sometimes you will come across annoying design faults such as taps under which you can't get a kettle, waterheaters which don't do the job, cupboards with faulty latches, light switches in the roof instead of at a sensible height and doors lacking catches on the inside. As far as the latter is concerned, it is sensible to have a small catch on the inside of your ramp so that you can lock it from the inside while parked at a show. There is little point in locking all the doors if thieves can drop a ramp and steal your tack.

By law you must have an access door through which you can gain admittance to the horses without lowering the ramp. This is a safety precaution as well as being convenient, but make certain that the door is in such a position that it cannot be undone by a horse. It is a great help, too, to have folding steps below the door. Nothing is more exasperating than to have to put clean tack on the lorry floor while you climb out and then have to pick it all up again. On wet days the tack will get filthy and all your hard work is for nothing.

It is also essential to have somewhere to store the tack while you are travelling and make sure that wherever it is the horses cannot reach out to snort on it, or even chew it. Some boxes have saddle racks set in such a position that you need to be a contortionist to retrieve saddles and bridles.

For long journeys there must be an area where you can store hay, feed and other equipment, while excess hay can be carried on the roof. Most modern boxes have racks built on

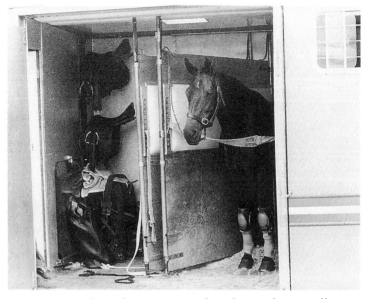

A box showing the tackroom next to the sideways facing stall

them for this purpose. Some are the full length of the vehicle, while others are shorter.

When you purchase a box, check to make sure that it has plenty of tie rings, not only for the horses but also for haynets. These latter rings should be set higher than the tie rings so that a net does not become entangled around a hoof if a horse paws.

Don't overlook interior lighting as it is absolutely essential when loading horses at night as they dislike entering a dark container. On the same subject, I like to have sidelights on top of the vehicle so that drivers of oncoming cars can judge the height and appreciate that you are much larger than an ordinary car.

It should not have to be emphasised that regular maintenance is essential. Keep a close check on your brakes, springs, tyres (don't forget a spare plus jack), wheel-nuts and lights. Always carry at least one fire-extinguisher; two is a sensible precaution.

Prices of horseboxes vary enormously. A guideline would be from £1,500 to £15,000, but large lorries such as those used for show-jumping can cost from £20,000 up to as much as £60,000. Much depends on the size, inside requirements, whether you build a container on an old or new chassis, and whether the body is constructed of wood, alloy or fibreglass. Most coach-builders will construct lorries up to 7½ tons which do not require an HGV licence or tachograph. If you are fortunate, you may come across a reasonably priced second-hand horsebox without using the service of a dealer, but if you convert one yourself make sure that you will remain within the law, especially regarding height and the weight you are allowed to carry. This subject is dealt with in Chapter 7.

Chapter
2

Rugs and Tack

2

When travelling your horse you will, naturally, wish to protect it from any potential injury, either through its own fault or as the result of an accident. It is also essential to protect and support the animal's legs while it is travelling. If there is a possibility of the horse injuring itself, however remote the likelihood, the animal will manage it somehow. It is also a fact that some horses are accident prone and will find a splinter or protruding nail if it is at all possible to do so.

Legs are precious so let's look at them first. There are a number of different types of leg-wraps and bandages on the market for leg protection. Leg-wraps are usually foam backed with Velcro fastening for easy application and removal. Some of these wraps are structured so that they provide knee- and hock-caps all in one. Leg-wraps are very useful for the experienced horse but can be a disaster with a youngster as the novelty of having strange bindings around its legs may cause it to panic, and if a fastening comes free and the animal treads on it, there will be trouble.

If you want to travel the youngster in boots and bandages then give it time to become used to them by putting them on in the stable long before it has to travel. It will probably hop around at first, lifting its legs high in the air. Be very careful when first putting them on that you do not get kicked.

The best form of leg protection is bandaging. Bandages are usually made from wool or cotton stockinette and are non-elastic. Many people forget that coronets need protection, so when bandaging you should place pads under the bandages. These are stronger than gamgee tissue and ensure that the pads go right down to cover the animal's hooves for maximum protection.

Knee-caps should also be used when travelling. They are fastened by an elasticated strap at the top where they should be fairly tight so that they cannot slip down over the horse's fetlocks, but not so tight that they restrict the circulation.

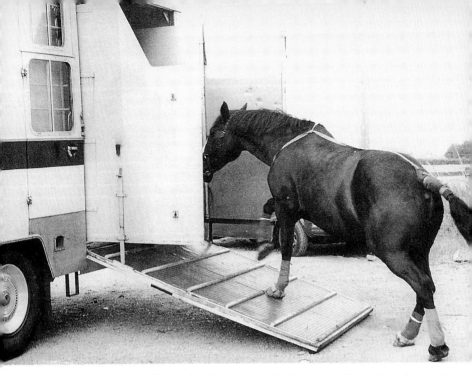

A Household Cavalry horse being loaded. Note the tailguard is tied without the use of a roller

The lower strap should be buckled loosely so that the horse can readily bend its leg. Hock-caps are applied in the same manner; however, sometimes it is better not to use them as they can irritate the horse and cause kicking.

Your horse's tail will need careful protection from rubbing. It should not be tightly bandaged around the bottom of the dock for if it is in place for several hours, the circulation can be restricted and this will kill the hair, causing it to fall out later. The bandage should not be put on wet. A tail-guard can also be fitted over the bandage in case it slips. Make sure it is made of very soft leather or strong but soft fabric otherwise it will rub into the tender skin at the top of the tail and make it very sore.

If you are going on a very long journey it would be wise just to fit the tail-guard and omit the bandage, otherwise it will probably slip and end up tangled around the horse's legs.

It is sensible to use poll-caps, for horses can become

extremely head-shy if they crack their heads in a trailer or lorry, or while they are being loaded or unloaded. The best type of poll-cap is the one which fits behind the ears and in front of the forelock with earholes. The headpiece of the headcollar fits through slots and it stays firmly in place. Not all the horseboxes and trailers are padded over the horses' heads, but the majority are padded along the sides to prevent bruising. If there should be no padding, then the use of rugs will help to protect the horse.

The number of rugs you travel the horse in is related to the amount it is wearing in the stable, whether or not it is clipped, the prevailing weather and how the horse travels. Of course, the more horses there are in a lorry, the warmer they will travel. It is not wise to travel a horse in a thick polyurethane rug or rug made from synthetic materials. You can, if you wish to make the horse look extremely smart, buy matching rugs, roller, tail-guard and bandages. However, if you do not want to go to so much expense, a jute rug is perfectly suitable for travelling the horse in as it is made of natural materials and will allow the horse's body to breathe should it get hot.

If your horse requires more than one rug on the journey, you should check it once or twice and if it seems to be too hot remove a layer. For this reason don't put the fillet string under the horse's tail as it will be difficult to remove a rug in the confined space of a box if it is in position.

If your horse is inclined to sweat whenever you travel it, possibly because it is nervously anticipating the event, then it may help to travel it with a sweat rug under its warm rug or fold the top corners of the top rug back under the roller (but keep checking it in case it slips back), thus giving the horse more air but still keeping the animal's loins warm. Obviously, if the weather is very hot, you will only need a cotton sheet or sweat rug at the most.

I learned one trick when travelling horses abroad which may be helpful if you have to remove a top rug. It was always extremely hot in the hold of the ferry even with all the box windows, doors and vents open and I found it far easier to attach the tail-guard to the roller on the first rug, sheet or sweat rug and put a surcingle on the second rug. This ensured that I did not lose the tapes or strap of the tail-guard or allowed it to slip down when I removed the top rug as it was firmly strapped in place by the roller.

If you are travelling the horse back from a competition it should be thoroughly cooled off before it is loaded. If the horse is just wearing a sweat rug when you leave the competition you should stop and check it after about half an hour as the animal may be feeling cold, perhaps as the result of a draught. If this proves to be the case, place a day rug over the top of the sweat rug. It also helps to relax the horse if it has a haynet to tear at on the way home.

Always make a practice of tying the horse up by the headcollar and never by the bridle. If it panicked and pulled back, the bridle would be smashed and the horse might also damage its mouth. It is preferable to leave the tack off the horse when travelling unless you are making a short journey. If, for instance, you are going hunting it will be more convenient to tack the horse up and place a headcollar over the bridle and rugs over the saddle. The animal will probably be fairly excited by the time you arrive near the meet, especially if it is tied up, outside the box or trailer and other horses or hounds are passing by. It is a common sight to see a loose horse cantering up the road, half-tacked up with its owner in frantic pursuit. Always place a rug over the saddle when travelling with tack on as the horse can easily scratch and damage the tack in the narrow confines of the stall.

Some horses have a tendency to chew through lead ropes when travelling and may break loose. If this is the case with your animal, you will have to use a chain which can be left attached by a piece of string to the ring in the box so that when you lead the horse into the box you can quickly clip the chain to the headcollar.

Do not lead the horse by a chain as, if it pulls back, your hand will be torn. If you are leading the horse with a bridle it is wise to put the headcollar on underneath the bridle so that you can quickly slip the bridle off when you get into the box

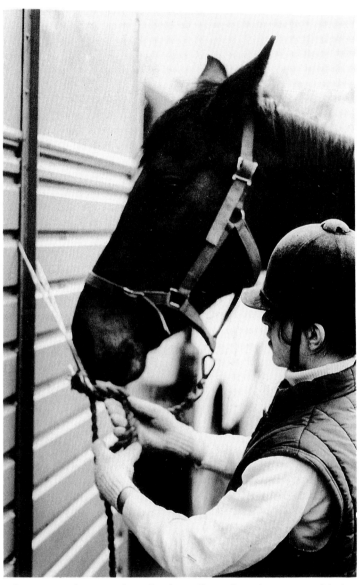

When tying a horse to the side of a trailer or box always use a binder twine loop which will snap if the horse pulls back and tie the horse up on the headcollar.

If the horse has a habit of chewing anything it can reach, make sure your smart rugs or other equipment are out of reach otherwise you may arrive at a show to find them in tatters. If the horse also tears at the padding in the box or trailer, it will have to be muzzled or you can fix a leather flap on the back of the nosepiece on the headcollar which will hang down behind the muzzle and effectively stop it.

It is always sensible to carry a few items of spare equipment on a journey such as a headcollar, bridle, rope, girth and leathers. The headcollar and rope may come in handy in case of a breakage and the bridle can be used if you have to unload the animal in a difficult place as you will be able to exert more control than with a headcollar and rope. At the same time you will not wish to use your best bridle. Spare girth and leathers are always handy – if only to lend to friends who have forgotten them or had the disaster of a break.

Never travel a horse or pony without a surcingle or roller over its rug as even on the shortest journey the rug will slip and the animal will trample on and almost certainly ruin it.

Another important tip is always to tie the horse to a piece of baler twine which has been attached to the ring so that if the animal does pull back it will break the string rather than the headcollar and rope and perhaps injure itself.

Common sense at all times is the key to successful horse handling and travelling. It is a virtue which could be applied with a great deal more energy than usually seems to be the case.

Chapter 3

Loading and Unloading

3

Loading – or rather not loading – probably causes more heartache, frustration, bad temper and abuse of horses than any other aspect of the equestrian world. Lack of common sense, irritation and sheer brutality are too often the hallmarks which result in a terrified animal, one which may take weeks or even months of rehabilitation before its confidence has been won. It is, when you think about it, asking a great deal of a young or inexperienced horse to walk into a relatively dark, narrow box and allow itself to be propelled at considerable speed.

If you know your horse may be apprehensive or difficult to load, then always allow plenty of time. Rushing the operation or frightening the animal through frayed tempers will only cause severe problems later on, even if you succeed in bullying the horse into the trailer or box. A horse does not think but is reliant on memory so it is essential to create good vibrations about loading and travelling.

Try to make the trailer look as inviting as possible to the horse. If the trailer has a front-unloading ramp it helps to open it so that the horse can see daylight from the loading side.

A horse will easily become frightened if the ramp moves when it places its hooves upon it. This usually occurs if the ramp has to be lowered on to rough or uneven ground. A brick or block placed underneath will help to steady it. With a trailer it helps to lower the jockey wheel and trailer jacks even though it may still be attached to the towing vehicle. In the case of a car this will prevent the suspension from bouncing which may make the horse lose balance and feel insecure. Make sure all these precautions have been taken before you bring the horse out to be loaded as the less time spent fiddling with the vehicle and trailer the better. The horse will become annoyed and upset at constant stoppages.

When approaching the trailer always walk beside the

The reluctant loader! It is not a good idea to pull the horse forward from the front

horse's shoulder. Never, under any circumstances, stand in front of its head and attempt to pull it forward. You will obscure its view and make the animal nervous, while if it plunged you would be in danger. The horse must not be frightened in any way by the person leading it but only receive encouragement or pressure from behind.

If your horse shows signs of barging, a headcollar will not be a sufficient control. The best type of instrument to use is a Chiffney bit, which is widely used in racing stables. If you prefer not to purchase this additional piece of tack, an ordinary bridle can be used, but it is not so effective as it will pull over the horse's teeth. However, if the horse displays signs of pulling back, it may be wise to attach a lunge rein to the bridle to ensure the horse does not break free. If the horse

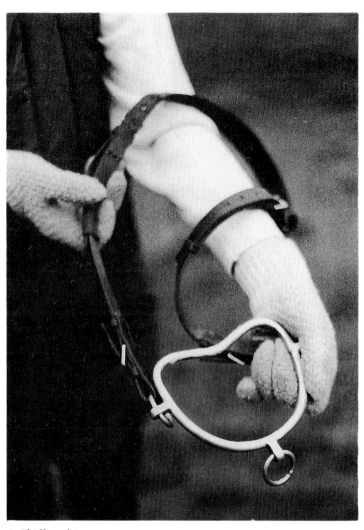

A Chiffney bit

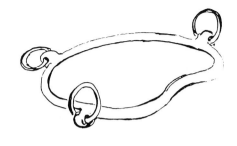

The Chiffney bit is used extensively in racing stables for reluctant
loaders, and to control young horses

Loading against a wall without the use of a lunge rein

does attempt to pull back, try to go with it rather than engage in a tug-o'-war session which will probably result in victory on its side, and possibly a damaged mouth.

If it is proving difficult to manoeuvre the horse on to the ramp, the answer is to place the box or trailer alongside a wall or thick hedge, thus providing a barrier on one side. A very narrow lane may also be of assistance in guiding the horse towards the ramp – provided, of course, you do not hold up traffic.

Food may also be used to entice the animal into the trailer or box, but if it is still unwilling to load you will need help from behind, but do try to ensure that the person or persons assisting you are experienced in handling horses. Nothing is more likely to lead to a disastrous situation than a nervous helper who panics at the last minute or starts to shout at the animal.

Always keep out of the horse's direct kicking line as if the animal panics or becomes aggressive it may well react by

49

First time in a trailer – and how *not* to do it. The lunge rein is on the wrong side, and the assistant could easily be kicked. Note that the trailer has been placed alongside a wall

The lunge rein is now on the right side, but the animal is still hesitant. The partition has been moved across

Walking forward freely now . . .

. . . and inside!

lashing out backwards. This warning also applies to the person leading the horse; standing directly in front of the animal is just as dangerous as being behind, for if it rears it could easily inflict severe injury. By the same token, should the handler be standing in front and the horse decides suddenly to charge into the trailer, the assistant might be badly trampled. If the horse is apt to rear, then a long rope or lunge rein should be attached to the Chiffney or bridle.

Often someone pushing from behind with the bristles of a broom will be sufficient to make the horse load. However, more pressure may be required and this can be applied by means of a lunge rein. If there is only one other person assisting you, you will have to tie the lunge rein to one side of the trailer. As the horse is led to the ramp by one person, the other walks behind, carefully drawing the lunge rein up at the back of the horse's quarters until one reaches the other side of the trailer. Then, by applying pressure and tightening and shortening the rein, the horse should be guided up the ramp and into the trailer. Do not flap or wave the lunge rein as this will frighten the animal.

If the horse is proving very reluctant to load, then at least two other people will be required to assist you. They should each take a lunge rein and attach it to the side of the trailer and, walking behind the horse as it approaches the ramp, they should cross the reins and pull them tightly behind the horse, so providing a much stronger human winch. It is advisable to wear a pair of gloves if you are holding a rope or rein to prevent burns and to offer more grip.

Another method of loading is to use a blindfold. These are frequently used by starters at race meetings but are not advisable for young horses, but only for mature animals which are set in their ways and unlikely to become head-shy. You must be extremely quiet and gentle when applying a blindfold to a horse as, if approached in a rough or boisterous manner, it could become badly frightened.

It may be necessary to walk the animal a couple of times in circles to disorientate it before you approach the ramp. When using this method of loading it is advisable to have someone

One method of using a lunge rein when there is no assistance. This is seldom successful with a really difficult loader

walking beside the horse with one hand on its quarters to reassure and guide it into the box or trailer. Talk in calm and encouraging tones to give it confidence.

There is now on the market a new gadget called the Easyloader which is designed to help you load your horse if you are on your own. Two comfortable handles are attached to a trace rope which runs right round the horse's body at trace height, giving control over the horse while loading, and a free-running carrier rope ensures the correct placing of the trace rope round the hamstrings. Pressure is applied on the trace rope according to the horse's response – a steady pull until the animal moves forward, or short, sharp jerks when it is in line with the opening. I have never used it myself but am told that it is simple and effective with the most stubborn horse, provided you stay calm and take your time.

Whenever you are loading a horse or pony make sure that

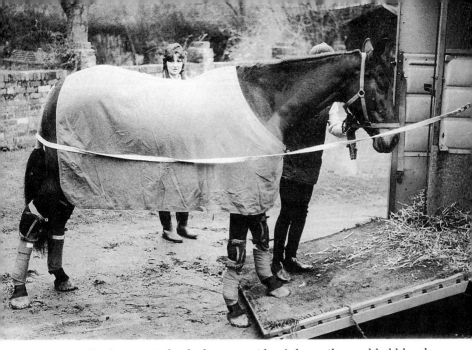

The lunge rein hooked on one side of the trailer, and held by the groom on the other side

The trailer parked against a wall, and the lunge rein used to keep the horse on the ramp

Lifting a leg at a time can sometimes work with a reluctant loader

the area in which you are parked is quite safe. If, for instance, you are loading from a field, take care that you are not close to wire or a ditch into which the horse could run if it panicked. Try not to load off a slippery tarmac surface or again, should the animal become upset or frightened, it could easily slip.

The area should also be clear of other vehicles as severe damage could occur both to the horse and machinery in the event of an accident. Particular attention should be paid to this point when using a blindfold for a horse unable to see where it is going may lash out in any direction and the handler may not be able to remove the blindfold in time.

If the horse appears simply anxious about the appearance of the box or trailer, then take your time and allow it to inspect the vehicle, the while patting and talking to the animal. At this point it may be helpful to lift one of the horse's hooves onto the ramp as a form of encouragement and to give it confidence in its stability.

One method of loading which is strongly to be condemned is riding a horse into a box. This is extremely dangerous. The

An extension to the ramp of a horsebox avoids the step, but it does make the ramp heavier

rider may become trapped and badly injured on the ramp gates or partitions, and if the animal rears he or she is bound to be hurt.

You may, on occasions, be lucky enough to have a 'loading ramp' in the form of a large bank against which the lorry can be placed and the ramp lowered on to it. It is advisable to have a pair of partitions between which the ramp may be lowered. The horse may then be led on to the bank, between the partitions and safely into the box. Alternatively, you may have a loading ramp constructed. This is built to the height of the horsebox floor at its highest point and slopes backwards to ground level. It should have filled-in fences at its sides which should, for preference, be solid to guide the horse into the box. This is often very helpful for loading as it creates the impression that the horse is walking on level ground; the slope is long and gradual, not short and steep like the lorry ramp.

One important point to note is that strong and boisterous ponies should only be handled by adults. An accident can easily occur to a child if a pony becomes stroppy.

Whatever method you decide to use, once the animal has been loaded tie it up fairly short so that it cannot reach another horse beside it. In most boxes there is a headboard to separate the animals, although this is rarely the case in a trailer. Make sure, however, that the horse has enough rope to reach its haynet but not enough to tangle it around its head.

Make a fuss of your horse or pony when it walks into the trailer or box and reward it with a handful of food. Secure the breeching straps and then raise and fasten the ramp. Check that all clips are secure, fasten the groom's door and the door over the front ramp in the case of a trailer. Also ensure that the doors above the back ramp are securely fastened when they are left open or closed. In the case of a trailer, wind up the jockey wheel and secure it. Check that both stabilisers are secure at the rear of the trailer.

The electrics plug must be firmly pushed into its socket and then check that all the trailer lights are working, including brake, side and indicators. Check that no wires or cables are trailing and, most important of all, ensure that the ball and tow-bar are firmly clamped together. Release the handbrake on the towing-bar and you are ready to move off. In the case of a box also check all the lighting and indicators.

Whatever method you use to load your horse or pony, try to take into account the animal's temperament, its age and any previous travelling experience. Above all, remain calm. Shouting, abusing the animal or hitting it will guarantee that it will never load in the future without severe problems.

Teaching the Young Horse to Travel

Before you consider loading and travelling it, certain points need to be considered if your horse is not yet broken. The elements of training must be carefully considered and undertaken before any attempt is made.

Assuming that the animal has at least been taught to lead, it must then be taught to tie up quietly in its stable. This can take place while you are grooming it or doing general stable duties. You will, of course, also wish to protect the horse's legs, so you must also get it used to having bandages and knee-caps on its legs. Again, this can be taught while you are daily attending to the animal. It is not advisable to leave the horse unattended when first applying leg wrappings as it may try to tear off the bandages with its teeth. It is also sensible to put a poll-guard on the horse to give it extra protection.

If you have a rear-unloading trailer you must teach your horse to back in the stable before you load it, quietly using your voice and placing one hand on the animal's chest to push it back a few paces until it becomes familiar with the movement.

When you first start to teach the young horse to load, make certain that you have two experienced handlers to help you. The box or trailer must be parked in a safe position with plenty of straw laid on the open ramp and inside on the floor. If you are using a box, be sure that the ramp gates and partition are safely pegged back. If you have a front-unload trailer, open the ramp to allow the horse to see through and have as much light and space as possible.

Now lead the horse out towards the vehicle and allow it to inspect the ramp, giving it plenty of time. Then encourage the horse to step onto the ramp. Your assistants should be quietly standing either side to help the horse to walk in a straight line. Walk beside the horse's shoulder, all the while talking in an encouraging tone as it walks into the box or trailer. If the animal displays apprehension the use of food to entice it may be of some assistance while at the same time the helpers should quietly pat the animal and encourage it from behind at a safe distance.

Once the horse is in the vehicle pat and reward it, but do not tie it up or put up the breeching straps or ramp. Give the horse food and allow it to stand calmly for a few minutes. If it tries to back out, do not pull it in the mouth but follow it out, while your assistant should try to guide it down the middle of the ramp, all the time calming it with use of the voice.

If, on the other hand, the horse seems to be taking things in its stride and is not upset, one assistant can undo the front breast-bars and you can walk the horse out through the front-unload door.

If the trailer is a rear unload, then quietly get under the breast-bar (be careful not to get trapped if the horse misbehaves) and start to push the horse backwards down the ramp, your helpers guiding it carefully until it is back on the ground. Do not at any time pull the horse in the mouth as it could throw its head and frighten itself badly.

If you have a horse-box, when you decide to lead the horse out an assistant should attach a lead rope to the far side of the animal so that when walking down the ramp it can be given support. On a steep ramp it could easily become unbalanced. This loading process should be continued for at least two or three days but it is up to you to assess how the horse is coping before you advance a stage further.

Once you are happy that the horse is completely calm about entering and leaving the trailer or box, you should be able to start putting up the ramp and tying up the animal. Still remain in the vehicle, rewarding it with food and allow it to stand there some time before unloading it. When you are satisfied that the horse is completely calm and in no way frightened about remaining in the box or trailer on its own, then you can take it for a short drive.

If you are using a trailer, after a short distance stop and let your assistant check that the horse is not distressed in any way. If the horse is travelling well, after taking it for a few rides you should be able to travel it safely at any time. However, it pays to practise the young horse at regular intervals to keep its training at a constant level.

Provided that the young horse has been correctly handled from an early age there should be no unnecessary problems connected with travelling. Once again, it is a matter of common sense and applying time and patience related to the horse's temperament.

Travelling Mares and Foals

Provided that your mare loads easily into a box or trailer, then the foal should follow quietly. When loading into a box the ramp will be far steeper than that of a trailer so make sure plenty of straw is placed on the ramp to prevent the foal from slipping on its rather long and unsteady legs.

In a box you may travel the mare and foal loose, but when using a trailer some mares should be tied up, otherwise they might try to turn round and crush the foal. This applies to big mares, which could become stuck. A pony mare should be quite safe. The partition in a trailer will have to be removed to travel a mare and foal as both parties will become very upset at being divided and the foal could be badly injured if it tries to climb the breast-bar to reach its mother.

At least one, preferably two, helpers should enter the box to hold the mare and particularly the foal before the ramp is lowered. This is very important, too, when using a trailer with a rear unload as you will not have a partition to prevent the foal from rushing forwards.

When unloading a mare and foal, place plenty of bedding on a steep box ramp to give the foal a grip and some protection should it stumble. If you have a front-unloading trailer it will be easy to unload both animals. If, on the other hand, it is a rear-unload trailer and the foal has turned round on the journey, take a firm hold of it while the ramp is being lowered then allow the foal to walk out. The mare may be anxious to follow her foal, but do not allow her to turn round and drag you out of the trailer. Keep her head facing forwards and push her back down the ramp.

If the foal seems unwilling to load, often two strong helpers linking hands behind the foal's quarters and giving a heave will be enough to pop it into the trailer. Strong people should deal with mares and foals as a mare may become very obstreperous if she is momentarily separated from her foal.

Do not travel mares and foals mixed with other horses as the foal could easily be trampled or attacked by a large or strange horse. Do not worry, though, if the foal lies down beside its dam as she will not trample on it.

When using a trailer to travel a mare and foal try to make sure that the vehicle has doors, or a grid, to close above the back ramp as, if the foal is loose and at all anxious about travelling, it could turn round and try to scrabble over the ramp with serious consequences.

If these simple guidelines are followed you should be able to travel your mare and foal perfectly safely and, provided the foal has a comfortable ride, it will have gained useful experience for later days.

Difficult and Problem Horses

Difficulties associated with travelling, loading and unloading horses or ponies can usually be identified as a result of poor or inconsistent handling and early training. So often owners will not take the time or trouble to study temperament or try to see matters through the animal's eyes. So many unthinking handlers simply assume that a horse is capable of reasoning in human terms whereas, of course, it basically reacts to stimuli and conditions.

A typical example involved transportation of two yearlings which I discovered were most unwilling to descend the ramp. It was not particularly steep but nothing I could do would persuade them to move forwards. It was quickly obvious that they had received virtually no handling and simply pulled back on their headcollars. In the end I had to resort to pushing them out with the bristles of my broom from the safety of the door of the living quarters in case they lashed out, while a handler held them in front, without pulling. Even then, to reduce the apparent slope of the ramp I had to find a raised grass verge which proved to be someone's garden. The latter's owner was not especially pleased but after an hour and a half of total frustration it proved the only answer.

One type of horse which can be singularly infuriating is the animal which likes to stand and kick for no apparent reason. Perhaps it wants to release pent up or nervous energy and finds that in a confined space kicking is the answer to its troubles, or perhaps it just likes to hear the sound of its hooves or shoes making expensive contact with wood or metal. One answer is to have an absorbent surface behind the horse so that the sound is deadened. Thick rubber matting over wood or metal may be of some assistance.

Once I was asked to travel a horse abroad, an animal which had acquired notoriety for kicking, so much so that it invariably cut its hocks to ribbons on a long journey. On this occasion we decided to glue a large piece of sponge about 6in (15cm) thick to the side of the lorry and directly behind the horse which was travelling sideways. Unable to hear itself trying to smash down the side of the lorry, it eventually gave up and arrived at its destination with hocks intact.

Persistent pawing and scraping is an unpleasant habit which can prove infuriating. A horse will usually engage in this vice when the horsebox or trailer is parked, rather than when it is on the move as then it is far too busy trying to keep its balance.

If there is a door directly in front of the animal over which it can place its head, pawing can result in a big knee, so if the horse does have this habit make sure it wears knee-pads and also protect the door with sponge rubber or some similar absorbent material if at all possible. If there is simply no other way to stop the animal, then the only answer may be to hobble the horse while the vehicle is stationary, but naturally the hobbles must be released before you drive off, otherwise the animal might collapse if you braked sharply or if it panicked. Also, do remember to take the hobbles off before trying to lead the horse from the box or trailer.

Some horses are expert escape artists and will somehow endeavour to extricate themselves from almost any enclosure, box, stable or trailer. I had heard stories of horses, quite large ones at that, escaping from trailer stalls or somehow managing to turn round and face backwards. I must confess that I treated such tales as being pretty tall until I was asked to take a horse with a Houdini reputation for a ride in my horsebox to try to cure his habit of escaping. He was, in fact, named Houdini as he had once managed to jump over

Leading a horse from a box. Note the litter on the ramp to assist grip

two stable doors and while in a trailer had clambered out of a stall, over the breast-bar and into the adjacent stall, all while the trailer was on the move. The incredible part is that he had damaged nothing in the trailer and had emerged quite unscathed. When he was led out the expression on his face clearly said: 'Aren't I a clever boy?'

I duly turned up at the horse's stable and led him into the front stall of my horsebox which faced sideways and also had a very high partition which was stronger than the usual type. As I drove away there was a terrific commotion inside the box and I wanted to stop to investigate, but the horse's owner was insistent that I keep on driving so that, when he realised he could not escape, the horse would eventually settle down. We drove for 10 miles (16km) and on several occasions the horrendous racket was repeated before, at last, and to my

Push against the horse's shoulder to steady it after a long journey when it may be stiff

Keep one hand on the shoulder when unloading to guide the horse down the ramp

relief, we turned back for his stable. All was now deathly quiet. 'He must have died,' joked his owner.

When we had parked in the stable yard I let down the ramp and looked along the floor under the partitions. 'He isn't dead,' I reported joyfully, 'I can still see all four feet.' Then a doubt struck me. 'Which stall did we put him in?' I queried. When we opened all the partitions the horse was standing in the second stall from the front with one scratch on his nose and a self-satisfied smirk on his face.

I simply could not believe it had happened and led the horse outside. As I stood on the ramp trying to work out how the partition was still standing, Houdini pricked his ears and started to walk back up the ramp. His experience had not frightened him in the least and he would have been quite content to go for another ride and perhaps show us a further trick!

Later we worked out how he had effected his escape. What he had done was to throw up his head and crack the roof, at the same time breaking his headcollar. He had then put his head through the groom's 'access pop-hole' in the partition and lifted it up. Both lower pins had popped out and the horse had then pushed underneath the partition which had swung to let him creep through like a rabbit under a fence. The partition was not broken although the iron hinges were bent and had to be straightened by the blacksmith.

I told the owner that I was filled with admiration for Houdini and that he would probably make a brilliant eventer. He was obviously so brave that he would stop at nothing. She agreed but, sadly, had to sell him as she simply could not contain him in a stable or field. I often wondered how his new owners coped. If you have a horse like that there is really only one answer – sell it!

Another particularly objectionable habit in a horse is barging. Once again it usually stems from lack of firm handling and discipline as a youngster. If a foal is handled from birth as it should be, it will never acquire such annoying, and sometimes dangerous, habits. Barging is a very difficult vice to cure once it is established. However, if the

Help the horse to back down the ramp when unloading

horse does make a habit of pushing and barging, the Chiffney bit, previously described, will help you hold and control the animal while giving it a sharp tap or two across the chest with a cane. This is not in any way cruel but simply a disciplinary reminder and is similar to a slap on a naughty boy's leg.

One thing to watch out for after a very long journey is stiffness in the horse. If the animal is weary and tired after spending a considerable time travelling, all of which will have been spent standing and balancing, the joints may well become stiff, so make sure that the horse does not try to rush down the ramp. Push against the animal's shoulder to steady it, otherwise it may crumple and collapse on the ramp. I once saw this happen to a racehorse after a long flight from abroad and a tedious horsebox journey. It cut itself severely on the tarmac in its trainer's yard and badly bruised its knees and hocks.

Chapter
4

Travelling

4

Towing

If you are going to tow a trailer then, as previously mentioned, it is far safer all round to use a Land-Rover, Range Rover or similar four-wheel drive vehicle in preference to a car. In my opinion, far too many people attempt to tow with a car which is too light for the trailer and then they wonder why the trailer overturns or their clutch burns out. For instance, a friend of mine told me that he was considering towing a very heavy wooden trailer which was to carry an extremely large horse plus trunk and feed and equipment, and all this with a lightweight Scimitar! Naturally, I advised him not even to contemplate it.

If you are in any doubt, check with your car manufacturer or dealer, either of whom will advise you on the car's maximum towing capacity. Make sure you use only a towing hitch recommended by the car manufacturer. Trailers and the weight they have to carry are enormously heavy and can exert tremendous pressure on a car. Remember, too, that if you intend to use a car you must be extremely cautious about where you park. Keep off verges, or at least have only two wheels on grass. If there has been any rain or the ground is sodden, the odds on your becoming firmly stuck are high.

The height of the towing hitch needs careful checking. The average trailer is 16½in (42cm) but this can vary. If the hook is too low or high on the car, the weight distribution will be affected by the trailer. It should ride evenly on both axles with two horses aboard to give a safe and comfortable ride. If the principal weight is over one axle you will then encounter pitching or snaking problems, or both, and perhaps burst tyres, while the horse, which will have had an uncomfortable ride, may be unwilling to reload.

If the trailer is higher in front than the rear the horses will press hard against the ramp and also badly rub their tails, but if the front end rides downwards your steering will not be

The ball-hitch
should be lower
than the tow-bar

Backing a Land-
Rover onto a trailer
with assistance

Use a checklist to confirm all the safety factors on a trailer

true. Drop plates and hitches can be used to correct the problem but have them fitted by an expert as extra bracing will be required. Always check your vehicle and trailer on level ground; the trailer should appear even or tilting very slightly downwards towards the ball.

I must confess that I find it quite amazing that one is not required to pass some form of test for towing caravans or trailers with a motorised vehicle. Pulling a caravan on its own can be bad enough, but the responsibility when you have a trailer containing live animals which can, to a certain extent, move, is far greater.

The great secret of towing for the first time is to remain calm and not panic. The first thing to do is hitch the trailer to the car or four-wheel drive and this, for the beginner, can be quite a demanding feat. If there is no one to assist you, you will probably have to make several attempts. There is no point in denting your number plate or knocking the jockey wheel off the trailer, so go slowly. A helpful aid is to place a marker, such as a stone, on the ground, so that you will know when to stop. With practice and experience you will find that you can judge the backing on to the trailer to a nicety.

Ideally, your ball-hitch should be lower than the tow-bar and you should be able to wind the latter up so that you can drop it on the ball. It is vital to make sure the catch is secure. Lift the trailer to be certain there is no movement. A friend, in a hurry and late for a meet of hounds, failed to wind the hitch down on to the ball, drove off and within a mile saw in the mirror, to his horror, the trailer parting company with the car and vanishing into a ditch. Fortunately, neither of the two horses was hurt but the front of the trailer was badly smashed.

Once you are sure the hitch is clamped tight, then plug in your lights, raise the jockey wheel and secure the safety chain. Good jockey wheels should have a spiral catch so that they cannot slip down while you are driving. That once happened to me and I arrived at my destination with a half-moon shaped jockey wheel!

It is essential to check the trailer lights every time you plug them in. If there is no one to help you, place a brick or heavy piece of wood on the brake pedal to check the brake lights. The lighting system on a trailer, unless the wiring is well protected, can quickly become damaged or corroded, so always keep a sharp eye open and make sure everything is working. Finally, before moving off do not fail to take off the brake on the trailer hitch.

When towing for the first time do not have animals aboard. You will need to get the feel of the trailer and appreciate the extra width you have to allow behind you, and the additional

Don't drive a trailer too fast, particularly on bends

burden of a horse to worry about is not required. You will have to take wider sweeps around corners than you would in a car and the best advice is to think of the car and trailer as an articulated vehicle. Do not forget that you are handling a unit which is longer than usual and allow for the trailer running in towards the corner. You will need to set your mirrors at an angle or purchase mirror extensions so you can see past the trailer.

Once you feel that you have mastered towing the trailer without a horse, to check your competence test yourself with a few heavy oil-drums inside the trailer. If they are still standing by the time you return home you should be able to drive with horses aboard.

One of the hazards of driving a trailer is that drivers of other vehicles, including lorry drivers, become very impatient when they get behind you. While it is important to give your four-legged passengers a smooth and comfortable ride, make every effort to let vehicles behind get past. This is important on a long journey when a queue may build up behind you. It is then considerate to stop at intervals in a lay-by to let the traffic past.

If you have to turn into a gateway, make certain that vehicles following behind understand your manoeuvre by making a clear signal in plenty of time. Execute the turn slowly. You will need a wide sweep to turn into a left-hand gateway, so don't let drivers be in any doubt, or imagine that you are turning right, otherwise you will find them creeping up your left-hand side just as you are about to turn. If you do not allow sufficient room for the turn you may find the trailer removing the gatepost.

It is important not to clash or jerk the gears or brake harshly as this will unbalance the horse and could throw it down, while if it panics it could turn the trailer right over. Remember to execute each move gradually and smoothly. If you are only carrying one horse, put it in the offside stall away from the lean of the camber, while if you are carrying two, ensure that the heavier horse is in the offside stall.

Your maximum speed should be 50mph (80km/ph), but this is only possible on motorways; 40mph (68km/ph) is more than adequate for other roads and considerably less on narrow, bendy lanes. If a straight route can be found, use it even if it entails a longer mileage. There will be less stress on the horse and driver. Remember to drive in low ratio gears downhill as well as up as this will save your brakes and reduce the risk of jack-knifing.

If you find you are going too fast downhill the trailer may start to snake from side to side. This is extremely dangerous and unless quickly corrected will result in the trailer twisting off the hitch and turning itself, and possibly the towing vehicle, over. If you feel the trailer starting to snake, reduce speed but do not brake sharply. Hold the steering wheel straight and as your speed lessens the snaking will stop. It is only caused by excessive speed.

Always approach traffic lights with caution. Even though they are green they may change at the last moment and then there is a temptation to slam on the brakes. Drive up to lights gradually so that there is time to slow down and stop if necessary. For the same reason never get too close to the vehicle in front – anticipate and always give yourself plenty of time.

When overtaking another vehicle, signal well in advance and pull out early. Try to keep as straight as possible until you pull in, again having signalled that you intend to do so. If you pull out and in suddenly this, also, can cause the trailer to snake and can be exceedingly dangerous on a motorway.

To keep a trailer stable when a large vehicle passes in the opposite direction, ease back slightly, then accelerate as you pass each other. You should not feel any movement as stability is maintained by actually towing the trailer at the moment of disturbance instead of just allowing it to cruise along behind you.

Take particular care on roundabouts. You won't be able to see much from the left-hand mirror, so it is better to keep to the left, even if you are going right round. You should be aware that lorry drivers can see little from their left-hand mirrors either. Even on the straight you will always have a blind spot right alongside you on the left. Drive very carefully when taking a roundabout as your horse can easily become unbalanced as you alter direction.

I recall once being asked why a horse was bad to load and, once aboard, whinnied all the time. I asked the driver if he drove steadily on bends and roundabouts and he assured me that he did. However, I agreed to go with him for a short journey to try to solve the problem. It became quickly apparent that the driver was taking the bends far too fast when cornering and the horse was whinnying in sheer terror. My idea of slow and that of the driver differed enormously! Always recall that your horse does not have hands to steady itself.

When you are driving on grass or rough tracks go very

slowly, as your front wheels will tend to bounce off the ground and the trailer will 'snatch' and jerk, giving the horse a very rough ride, apart from doing your car very little good.

Reversing

It is a simple fact that you should not drive a trailer on the road until you have mastered the art of reversing. Unfortunately, for some folk the sheer idea of trying to reverse seems to paralyse common sense. It is not difficult and once you have got the hang of it you will wonder what all the fuss was about.

The simplest method of learning is to take the towing vehicle and trailer into a field or large yard where there is plenty of open space and little likelihood of your backing into a house, stable or garage. To help you practise, use straw bales or cones as guidelines, and it is less embarrassing if you are on your own!

Start with the car or four-wheel and trailer in a straight line, and then decide which way you want the rear of the trailer to turn first. It is simpler to go to the right as you can

Practise reversing using markers as a guide

watch that side from your driving seat. Your vision is more restricted on the left as you only have the wing-mirror to aid you.

If you go to the right, reverse very slowly, gently moving the steering wheel to the left until the trailer begins to turn. Alter your steering wheel back to the right, noting how sharply the trailer is turning. If it is not turning sufficiently, again move the wheel to the left. If, however, it is turning too quickly and the angle is becoming too acute, move the steering wheel to the right. Drive slowly all the time until you begin to get the feel of it.

Always avoid turning too sharply when using full lock and never move too quickly as, almost inevitably, this will cause the trailer to jack-knife. If this does happen, simply pull forward until the car and trailer are in a straight line and start again. Do not try to correct a sharp angle by further reversing as this will only make matters worse and your car will acquire a dent and possibly lose its rear lights.

The great secret of reversing is to make every movement small and slow until you get the hang of it. Suddenly it will all come together and then, with further experience, you will discover that you can reverse a trailer into the tightest space or manoeuvre it almost onto a sixpence.

Vehicles and trailers move differently according to the length of the vehicle and sleeving lock and the length of the trailer and position of its axles. One thing to watch for is that you do not 'over-ride' on the clutch, otherwise you will damage it. A nasty acrid smell will warn you of trouble in this quarter, so stop for a while. Incidentally, reversing lights are extremely valuable at night.

It is absolutely essential to know how to reverse in an emergency. If you are stuck on soft ground or on a hill, don't be tempted to unhitch, particularly when loaded, as the trailer will be far too heavy to manoeuvre, nor does its handbrake operate if it is moving backwards. If you want to try the cheat's way out, get out and stand around looking helpless. Hopefully, someone will come to your rescue and show you how easy it all is. Many are the faint of heart who have driven miles further than necessary rather than attempt to reverse and turn round.

Another problem you are certain to encounter at some stage, especially if you attend shows regularly, is becoming bogged down in mud. Before you enter a show-ground, and assuming the surface is damp or it is raining, engage four-wheel drive if your vehicle has it, and put it into a low gear so that you do not have to change gear in the mud.

Don't follow in other vehicles' tracks as it will be even more slippery or the ground will be churned so deep that the underside of the vehicle and trailer scrape over the ground between the ruts. Under these circumstances your exhaust, oil sump, brake linkage and jockey wheel can become clogged with mud and will need a thorough clean to avoid their seizing up.

If you use too much throttle the wheels will start to spin, but on the other hand you must not drive too slowly in a very low gear as you will then lose propulsion. Front-wheel drive cars can sometimes gain traction by turning the steering wheel to left and right, while rear-wheel drive cars can be assisted by placing additional weight in the back. However, while all this is going on your horse may be having a rough ride in the trailer. It is probably far better to unload it,

A familiar sight! Jacknifed and embedded in mud

provided it is safe to do so. This is where a passenger can be of great assistance, but even if you are on your own, don't panic. There are bound to be other folk in the same predicament and help will soon be to hand.

If there is a tractor available take advantage of it before you get yourself into further trouble, but do watch where the driver hooks the chain. Bumpers and steering rods are definitely not suitable. If you are badly stuck, the wheels are spinning and there is no tractor to hand, you will have to provide some form of surface tension by placing material under, behind and in front of the wheels. Straw, wood, branches or sacks can all be used.

If even this fails the only answer is to unhitch the trailer and to drive the vehicle on to hard ground. However, make sure the trailer is empty and not on a slope where it can trundle off. With assistance you will probably be able to push or pull it out of the mud. It is advisable to carry with you a strong rope at all times as you never know when it may come in handy.

When at last you are back on the road, don't forget to check your tyre treads as they will be packed with mud and as well as being dangerous for other motorists following you, if you brake you may well go into a skid.

Sooner or later you are bound to have a puncture. This always happens at the most inconvenient time. Normally it will be in the dark, miles from anywhere, with a full load of horses and pouring with rain. This is the sort of occasion when you will thank your lucky stars that you have kept your spare wheel and tyre in good condition. Make sure that you always carry a wheel brace and tommy bar which will fit the nuts. Some garages today make a practice of replacing nuts with a pressure nozzle and they are almost impossible to remove by hand, so check before you get into trouble.

If your trailer has obsolete wheels and no spare, you should carry a spare tyre and tube. You might be miles from the nearest garage, and few of them carry stocks of trailer tyres. You should also make a note of the size of wheel and type of tyre.

Your jack should be of 2 tons capacity. If you have to change a wheel on the trailer, place the jack under the chassis of the trailer on one of the corners, next to the flat tyre, making sure you do not trap any electric wires.

If, on the other hand, you find yourself without a jack (and you shouldn't) a wedge-shaped block of wood at least 3in (76mm) thick should do the trick. Drive the good trailer wheel (on the punctured side) on to the block and this should raise the trailer sufficiently for you to raise the damaged wheel. Don't forget that the wheel nuts must be loosened before the trailer is lifted, otherwise the wheel will merely spin when you try to turn them. When you replace the nuts tighten them twice, loosely the first time and very tightly the second, top to bottom and diagonally so that even pressure is exerted on the rim. It is, of course, essential to carry a torch. Changing a wheel by touch in the dark is not easy.

How do you know when you have a puncture? If the trailer feels at all strange, begins to jerk or exert pressure on the towing vehicle, stop at once and examine the wheels. If you leave it too long, the tyre may be ruined, heat up or the rim will be damaged. For safety's sake, try to pull into a lay-by or hard shoulder on a busy road or motorway and immediately put out a warning red triangle as well as switching on your hazard lights.

I was once towing a borrowed trailer behind a borrowed horsebox and felt no sway or vibration when a wheel actually dropped off the trailer and bowled across the road in front of busy traffic, stopping at the central barrier. It was not until a taxi driver drew alongside and shouted that I realised something was amiss. Fortunately, the horse in the trailer didn't panic and stood patiently while we replaced the wheel which had fallen off because the nuts were loose. I learned to check borrowed equipment after that.

The trailer will also feel strange and heavy if the brakes have seized up, or the handbrake is left on and the hubs overheat, or when wheel bearings become slack. Hot, expanding grease in the hubs will force off the grease cap and hub-caps. The bearing can shatter and then the wheel will wobble until it falls off. If you hear any peculiar noises or are not happy with the way the trailer is handling, always stop and look.

Personally, I am hopeless when it comes to changing wheels so I always make a practice of carrying loose change for a telephone and protective clothing in case I have a long walk to the nearest box or house.

Your tow-bar nuts and bolts and the ball on your car or four-wheel vehicle should be checked regularly for wear and tear. Stand on the ball to see if the tow-bar flexes and if you hear any strange scraping noises, check to see if the tow-bar has worked loose. Trailers (and caravans) have too often been known to part company. This is where your safety chain will prove its worth.

Something else to be aware of is the height of the trailer. Drive very carefully and slowly if, for instance, you are in a narrow, tree-overhung lane as the noise of branches hitting the roof can easily frighten a horse, while you might also end up with a dented roof.

Many of the points and tips given apply both to trailers and horseboxes, but whichever you are driving or towing you must always anticipate what might happen – be alert and prepared for trouble at all times.

Summing up, you must never drive so fast in a built-up area that you cannot stop smoothly and comfortably without sudden braking. Be very wary of traffic lights changing at the last moment, use low gear downhill and ignore impatient drivers using their horns behind you, although pull in and let them pass whenever reasonably possible. Sadly, today all too many drivers of cars and lorries fail to understand that horses can only balance by standing and that a steady, smooth ride is essential to their welfare.

Horseboxes

A horsebox is higher than a trailer, so even more care is called for when driving under branches or garage forecourts which are roofed. Know the height of the vehicle so that when you

Watch out for overhead hazards when driving a box

encounter a low bridge with the clearance indicated on it, you will know whether or not you can safely drive underneath. It is always safer to drive under the centre of an arched bridge but remember to switch on your hazard lights as car drivers may not appreciate your manoeuvre. If you are not sure you can make it, drive right up to the bridge, stop and have a look. This will undoubtedly annoy anyone following behind you but will save a lot of damage and inconvenience for all concerned if you are too high. On more than one occasion I have only just scraped through when carrying bales of hay on the roof.

If you have to reverse away from a bridge or any other hazard, such as an accident, make sure drivers behind know what you are doing as you may not be able to see them. I once backed into a car at a low bridge and was accused of not looking in my mirror. I explained to the lady driver that mirrors can't see through wood. She was right behind the centre of the back ramp and invisible in either wing-mirror. Nevertheless, it cost me a bumper as it was my fault for not checking to see if anyone was there.

If you have a passenger with you it is always advisable for

Check brake, lights, safety-chain and jockey wheel before moving off

him or her to stand behind and direct you. At night reversing lights are essential, otherwise you will see nothing and the engine usually drowns any shouts, unless your assistant has a very loud voice. It is not always easy to judge how far to go as the length of the horsebox can appear distorted.

On motorways reasonable speed is immaterial to the horses you are carrying, although it may not appear so to a patrol car. When you are driving in a straight line horses will scarcely move but when you are back on bends and curves you must reduce your speed considerably. Most horses will adapt to travelling forwards, backwards and sideways provided they are driven sensibly and with consideration. You will find that a lorry is easier to drive than a car towing a trailer, particularly so if it is power-steered.

Punctures on horseboxes are, .naturally, a far bigger problem than on a trailer as the wheels are so much larger. I was once asked if I could change a wheel on a horsebox. The answer was simple: 'I can't even lift one up never mind change it!'

It is even more difficult if the inner tyre at the rear of the lorry has to be removed, as the outer wheel will have to come off first. For this reason it is vital to carry a really heavy jack to bear the weight and don't forget the lorry is much heavier with horses and equipment inside.

My worst nightmare in this respect was having no jack for a 14-ton weight when an inner tyre at the rear burst in the wilds of Bulgaria. I had six horses on board. We took the back three horses off and wedged the lorry precariously on a pile of stones on the edge of a river bank while three men changed the inner wheel.

It should not have to be emphasised that whether you drive a trailer or horsebox you must carry a tool-kit, spare engine oil, water for the horses and radiator and distilled water for the battery. If you run on diesel, do not let your tank become empty otherwise the whole system will have to be bled before you start again. Check your fuel gauge regularly to make sure it is working.

It is essential to have your horsebox serviced regularly at the correctly designated intervals and have it completely checked over if it has been laid up for the winter. Finally, check your lights and indicators regularly also and keep them free of mud.

Chapter 5

Accidents and Emergencies

Accidents involving trailers are, sadly, all too frequent and are far more common than they are with horseboxes. They are, time and again, caused by excessive speed and an inability to comprehend the dangers occasioned by towing one or two large, potentially nervous, animals on the highway.

Jack-knifing, mentioned in the previous chapter, can be caused by the camber of the road, by downhill braking, by taking bends too fast or by swaying caused by excess speed or being passed too closely by larger vehicles. This last is a particularly unpleasant and very common occurrence on motorways. Drivers of lorries or coaches seem incapable of appreciating the massive air disturbance created when they speed past a slow upright trailer. It is essential, on motorways, to watch the offside wing-mirror and to anticipate the air displacement as each large vehicle hurtles past.

Cross-winds on motorways, exposed roads and bridges can have a similar disturbing effect. Anti-sway bars connecting trailer and towing vehicle are available, but very few people seem to take advantage of them.

Whenever possible, travel with an assistant for, in the event of an accident, one may have to go and telephone while the other looks after the horses.

Even if your trailer does overturn, your car or four-wheel vehicle may still remain on its wheels. Although you will be shocked, think of your horses which will be lying on their sides or even upside down. One horse may be lying on the other and equipment may have tumbled on to them, to say nothing of the heavy partition.

Your first action must be to warn other drivers who may be following behind you. You must always carry red warning triangles and these should be placed at least 50yd (46m) in front of the accident. Ask someone to slow or, if necessary,

A trailer accident. Note the red warning triangle

stop all traffic while you attend to the horses. If the road is not blocked the majority of drivers will pass by as if nothing had happened and will be desperate to make sure they do not become involved. The excuse is usually that they would not know what to do about the horses anyway.

If it is impossible for you to extricate the horses from the trailer until help arrives, try to keep the animals calm. This may be very difficult, much depending on how badly they are trapped or injured, but you must try to prevent further injury caused by thrashing about. Hopefully, police, firemen and if necessary, an ambulance will have been telephoned without delay; the firemen may have to cut open the trailer before the horses can be released. It is also usually essential for a veterinary surgeon to be summoned.

If a horse is bleeding badly from a cut or cuts a tourniquet may be required, especially as it may be some time before the vet arrives. For this reason it is absolutely essential to carry plenty of crêpe bandages in your first aid kit. Note that you should always carry a kit which caters both for humans and horses. If your horse is very badly injured, the vet may have to destroy it.

In attempting to assist your horse or pony, whether in a trailer or horsebox, there is a great danger of becoming trapped by rolling bodies or hit by threshing legs. Be extremely cautious as unnecessary injury to yourself only causes further delays and problems.

If the animal is able to stand and walk about when released from trailer or box it will then have to be loaded onto a rescue vehicle, which will probably have been summoned by the police who will have telephoned the nearest haulier or stables. Leading a terrified horse on a motorway under these circumstances is extremely dangerous, but it has to be done.

A few years ago the British Horse Society conceived a Motorway Rescue Scheme which was administered by their county committees in close cooperation with the Motorway Police who, incidentally, welcomed the project with enthusiasm. The scheme began in the M6 country. Lancashire was first, then Cheshire and Staffordshire, and there are plans to extend the scheme throughout the country.

If you have an accident on a motorway do not attempt to unload the horse(s); your first move must be to telephone the Motorway Police – but be very careful when doing so. Don't wander about the lanes, and avoid stepping into the slow, or nearside, lane from the cab of a broken-down vehicle if it is parked on the hard shoulder. Make sure all your passengers and any dogs are safely out of the way of oncoming traffic.

When phoning, be precise with your details; state whether you are heading north, south, east or west and how far past the last junction you are. State the number of people and horses involved, your destination, the cause of the breakdown or details of the accident. Don't neglect to provide relevant information for a vet if he has to be called.

In areas where the Motorway Rescue Scheme applies the police hold a list of rescuers and vets for each junction. Rescuers are supplied with safety jackets and a horsebox sticker to aid police identification. They work as a team of two, never alone, and have back-up assistance available if required. Usually a patrol car will assess the situation and full police assistance will be provided, including their surveillance, if it is necessary to load your horses onto a rescue horsebox.

Every effort is made to get you moving again, but if an accident calls for both veterinary and breakdown facilities, then the horses are either taken to their home stables, or on to their destination or given suitable shelter. If essential, they will be taken to a veterinary hospital. The rescue horsebox will park in front of your trailer or box so that horses may be led along the verge in the same direction as the flow of traffic. This is where a bridle is essential as you cannot afford to let horses escape on the motorway.

You will be asked to sign a form indicating your willingness to be held responsible for any fees incurred, such as veterinary or breakdown services, plus a nominal charge for the rescuer's diesel – unless, of course, he is professionally engaged in the haulier business or entitled to charge for his services.

Maintaining a scheme of this nature demands time, effort and constant supervision by the BHS committees involved, but in these days of busy traffic it is both worthwhile and necessary. The BHS deserves full support for administering this excellent scheme.

An interesting observation on crashes and their results was made by Dr Sharon Cregier, who is Vice-President of the Canadian Wild Horse Society, North American Editor for *Equine Behaviour* and Chairman of the Canadian Committee on the Transport of the Horse. She is very much in favour of the rear-facing trailer and says:

> Once the horses are properly installed in the rear-face trailer, if the trailer is forced to an uneven or sudden stop, the horses' plump rumps instead of their fragile heads, come into contact with the bulkhead. Under most braking conditions the horses usually lean automatically away from the point of impact – an effortless inclination over the forequarters . . . In addition, such placement of the horses maintains a steady weight on the rear of the braking tow vehicle, assisting in stopping without upsetting the horses and minimising the danger of jack-knifing.

To emphasise the same point made above, I quote a report from a gentleman in New Zealand who was involved in a serious accident on a very narrow, hilly road. A 60ft (18m) tractor-trailer which was travelling too fast jack-knifed and hit the front of his rear-face Kiwi Safety Trailer. The front of the trailer was holed and two of its four wheels ripped off. However, the two trotting horses being carried had no injuries and remained calm in the trailer for several hours until a replacement trailer arrived. If they had been travelling in a conventional trailer they could have taken the full force of the impact and possibly even smashed through the front of the trailer.

Sometimes a trailer is overturned because a horse panics from claustrophobia. It will frantically scrabble at the floor

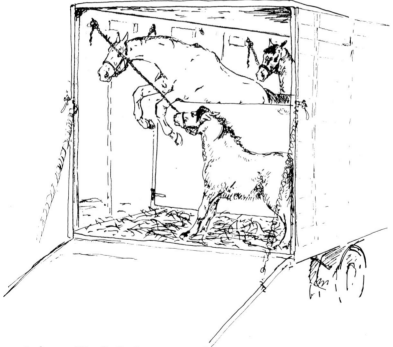

A horse Houdini! Some animals are adept at escaping and clambering over partitions

with its hooves and try to climb the breast-bar or partition. If your horse does scrabble, even though the trailer remains upright, you may have to accept the fact that you simply cannot tow it in a trailer. The only answer then is to travel it in a box. I have had, on many occasions, to transport 'scrabblers' and have never had any trouble with them in a horsebox. In such situations it helps if you can provide them with a wide stall in a box, for although they may not necessarily stand with legs splayed out, the effect is purely psychological and seems to work. Some horseboxes which carry the front horses three abreast and facing forward have the same problem of scrabbling if the animals are all big horses. Then it is sensible to place only two in wide stalls. It is interesting to note that some of the well-trained and disciplined horses of the Household Cavalry and King's Troop, RHA require wide stalls, and when they are picked up by a fleet of large horseboxes for a tattoo or display the drivers are told beforehand how many wide stalls will be required.

Horses which scrabble or climb can create extremely tricky situations, either ending up on the floor of the box or trailer, or trying to jump the partition or breast-bar, causing damage to themselves and the container. The next time the animal is required to travel after such an unpleasant experience it may be reluctant to load, and who can blame it? On the other hand, I've known horses which have turned over in a trailer, walk out of the roof without a scratch and which have gone straight on to load into a horsebox as if nothing has happened!

If your horse collapses through colic or some other sudden illness while in transit, you must first try to drive to the nearest place where help might be obtained, or at least to a telephone. In such a case speed is of the essence, as it can mean the difference between life and death. Fortunately, such occurrences are extremely rare.

Occasionally, a partition can work loose, or be kicked, so that it falls on a horse. I recall a terrible accident which occurred in a large ten-horse articulated vehicle carrying polo ponies which were well used to travelling. The driver had stopped in the yard to pick up some equipment when one of the ponies, in the middle of the container, went berserk. The spring bolts at the top and bottom of the partition sprang out of their holes and the partition fell on the horse which thrashed and kicked on the floor. This upset the other horses, all of which started to panic so that nearly all the partitions fell like a pack of collapsing dominoes. By the time the ramp was let down the scene inside the container was like the aftermath of a battle, with blood spattered everywhere. The horse which had initiated the panic was so badly injured it had to be destroyed, two others received severe injuries which took many months to heal, while the remainder had to be treated for cuts and bruises. That was a freak accident but shows how easily a tragedy can strike with little or no warning. This is when it pays to insure your horse or pony, as well as the box or trailer.

I mentioned earlier the need to make absolutely certain that the floor of the box or trailer is sound, yet one still hears reports of animals 'losing' a hoof, or more than one, through the collapse of rotten floors. They stand more chance of surviving if they are in a box, of course, as it is much higher off the surface of the road than the floor of a trailer. If you do have the misfortune to encounter such an accident you may have to saw or hammer pieces of wood out of the way to release the horse, but be careful when you do so in case the animal panics and kicks you.

Although I have never had to saw a horse out of the floor of a box or trailer, I always carried a saw with me in my box and had to use it on several occasions to extricate the roof-rack from overhanging branches.

It would, of course, be much easier to get horses out of an overturned box if all boxes had back ramps, even if the loading and unloading was done using a side ramp. In the case of a roll-over accident, the horses would be trapped; the side ramp would either be beneath them or above them, with no chance of getting them out at all. A back ramp, however, could save the day. Another possible advance in box design could be a roof which could be dismantled in sections, so avoiding the need to cut through the roof to let the horses out; the horses inside can easily be injured during this operation.

If your horse has fallen through the floor of a trailer while in transit it will stand very little chance and will almost certainly have to be destroyed, so it is in your own interests to inspect the floor regularly and to keep it clean.

Some of the accidents one hears about are almost incredible. In 1985 a horse fell out of a box when the ramp collapsed directly onto a following car, killing both itself and the driver. I repeat my exhortation – be safe at all times. You may only get one chance.

Accidents can also be caused if a horse kicks and succeeds in loosening the rivets on the metal lining of a trailer. If the lining comes away it can all too easily rip the horse's leg. This happened to the horse of a friend. She heard the animal kicking, but was driving in heavy traffic on a very busy main road and as she did not have far to go she carried on. When she came to unload the horse in pouring rain she discovered blood pumping from a cut artery in a leg. Fortunately, she was able to apply a tourniquet. The vet came at once and stitched the deep wound. He later told me that the horse had lost so much blood that he doubted if it could survive. However, survive it did but that was one lesson learned the hard way.

Linings on modern vehicles and trailers are now often constructed of material such as thick rubber which, of course, cannot cause cutting injuries, but many are still metal lined and need careful inspection.

Other road users seldom seem to be aware of what can happen when live animals are contained in a horsebox or trailer. Horses, in particular, tend to be highly strung and neurotic and can all too easily be upset. It is infuriating when thoughtless drivers blow their horns behind you and again when they pass. Something to curb this would be a compulsory notice on all livestock trailers and boxes carrying the message: 'Please avoid using horn. Pass with care. Horses/cattle/livestock in transit.' The usual notice 'Caution horses in transit' is pointless as no one understands what they are expected to do, or not to do.

Finally, do try to undertake everything carefully and calmly. There is absolutely no point in rushing; if you are running late, hasty driving will only result in exhausted and upset horses, or, at the very worst, an accident. Remember that most accidents can be avoided with care and forethought.

It is almost superfluous to mention alcohol, but if you are drinking don't drive. The hunting field is one occasion when a considerable amount of drink can be available and it is surprising how much one can take aboard from the kindly offering of flasks throughout the day. Be warned and know your own capacity.

Chapter 6

Hints for the Journey

6

The amount of planning required for a journey must, obviously, depend on the length of time you will be away. If you are making a short, out and back home in one day, trip then you will not have to involve yourself with detailed planning of rations for human and horse. On the other hand, there are basic requirements which cannot be overlooked.

It is essential to plan your route well in advance. If it is new ground, obtain a map and try to avoid long stretches of winding, narrow country lanes and steep hills. Watch out for low bridges. It is far preferable to take a longer route on clear dual-carriageway or motorway than to get snarled up in minor roads where, if there is an obstruction and you have to turn, there may well be severe problems. The longer route is likely, in the end, to prove faster. If you are in any doubt contact the Automobile Association who will give you every assistance with route planning.

The amount of food and equipment for your horse and yourself will, as mentioned above, depend on the duration of your journey and how long you will be away. If you are going to a show and returning on the same day you will only require the horse's normal feed ration plus a couple of haynets. It is essential to have water in plastic carriers, not only for the animals but also for a radiator should it become thirsty or a fan belt breaks. You may also need water to wash yourself should you become covered in grease and oil following a breakdown.

If, on the other hand, you are going to be away for a few days at a show or event, you will have to calculate with care exactly how much feed and hay to take with you. Even when you think you have got it right always add a little more to cater for an emergency. Should your vehicle break down it may take more than a day to effect repairs, so you need to be prepared.

Before setting out be absolutely certain that the tank is

filled up, whether diesel or petrol, and never take a chance on finding a garage. Carry a can of spare fuel, but remember that the law specifies that certain types of container are illegal.

I always like to carry some form of handy refreshment on a long journey, such as sweets or fruit. Finally, be certain you have change available in case you have to make a phone call in the event of an emergency.

If you are going to undertake regular trips away for several days at a time, then, if you drive a horsebox and have limited space inside, it is well worth having a roof-rack built on top of the box. The size can be adapted to the number of bales of hay you are likely to require at any one time but you will also need a waterproof sheet to cover the load. This must have strong ropes attached otherwise it will take off on its own.

On very long journeys always check your horse at regular intervals and offer it a drink. It will not invariably want one but is more likely to do so after eating hay. Never allow it to drink too much water at once, especially in cold weather – little and often is the ideal. This applies to the end of the journey as well. Don't let the horse gulp down a couple of bucketsful at its destination; you should allow half a bucket and then more later on.

When tying up the haynet make sure that the horse cannot get its hoof in the netting should it paw or scrape. Many people forget that as a net gradually empties so it also lengthens and drops, so instead of fastening the drawstring loop through the tie-ring and back on to the loop, fasten the loop on to the bottom of the net so that it cannot drop any further. This is elementary Pony Club training, but so few people give it a thought. Make sure, too, that the net is securely tied, otherwise if it comes off the tie-ring you will find the horse with the net enmeshed around its legs.

You should always have a small amount of hay for the animal to nibble at on its journey, unless it is going to work hard straight away, otherwise if it is hungry on arrival it will guzzle anything in sight, including its bedding and give itself colic. It is amazing the number of people who do not feed their horses while they are in transit. Horse transporters for the meat trade are particularly at fault in this respect.

You are probably unlikely to be involved in sea crossings, an exercise which I have undertaken on numerous occasions, but if this should befall you make absolutely certain the horse has plenty to eat. Customs frequently hold up the lorries for several hours and the final road journey to its destination can be the last straw if the animal is hungry. It will be positively starving when it gets there and will take longer to recover.

Fortunately, show-jumpers usually travel very well on long journeys as they are hard and fit and used to them, while at the same time they are constantly watered and checked by their grooms. It is interesting to note that they are less worried by the noise of traffic than most other horses. Many show-jumpers travel sideways and the grooms can attend to them by crawling in front of them under their headboard. The horses soon become used to this when they know it means food or titbits.

Rugs can, and should be, changed according to temperature as previously mentioned. In this respect, I recall an appalling incident which illustrates the need to check rugs regularly and not to take chances.

The animal involved was a French horse which had jumped in the last class at the Berlin show but had not cooled off properly. Instead of resting the horses overnight, for some unaccountable reason the driver of the German articulated lorry decided to leave as soon as the show had ended. The horse was loaded, still sweating and too warm to be rugged up correctly. Half an hour later the groom wanted to put another rug on the horse, but the lorry was designed so that there was only access to the front horses which faced forwards. However, the French horse was further back and to reach him meant stopping the lorry. The driver refused. It was a bitterly cold night and the horse was eventually unloaded many hours later trembling with cold and within a short period had died of pneumonia.

No matter how rushed you may be for time your horse always comes first. When travelling really long distances it is a good plan to carry a thermometer in your first aid kit so that you can keep a close eye on the horses' temperatures which, ideally, should be 100°F (37.7°C).

Be very wary of going into a stall to check rugs while someone is driving as a horse could easily tread on you or crush you unintentionally against a partition, while trying to keep its balance. It is far safer to stop and then attend to the horses.

If there are no access doors and you have to climb round to get in to the horses, again never attempt this while the vehicle is moving. A few years ago a teenage girl did just this but fell under a pony and was trampled to death. Her screams were not heard in the cab.

It is both illegal and highly dangerous to travel in a moving trailer – the same rule applies to a caravan – so you will have to stop if you want to check your horse. Every time you stop for fuel, meals or for any other reason, automatically check the animal to make sure all is well and that it is comfortable. A stop will also give it a chance to stale. Some horses will not stale in the box or trailer if there is an absence of straw as the lack of bedding seems to discourage them. If you are undertaking a long journey you must make a break and lead the horse out. This is not always as easy as it sounds for there are remarkably few places where it is safe to lead a horse around off the road. The problem will be magnified if you are carrying three or more animals and have only one person to assist you, particularly if there is a bad loader among them. If there is likely to be a major problem leave the horses on board – there will be less stress all round.

Some years ago I took three horses abroad, one of which was a mare which adamantly refused to stale in the lorry. We stabled during the journey, but on the last night had no stabling so we took all three out for a walk behind a garage where we had bought diesel. There the mare relieved herself to the sound of pleasurable grunts, much to the astonishment of an Italian goat-herd minding his charges close by, and who had not seen the mare approach him.

On another occasion I travelled as co-driver and groom to

Spain with a load of seven horses, five of which were two- and three-year old thoroughbreds which had very little previous experience of travelling. We were short of stabling on the journey and four of the colts were such unruly and bad loaders that they never came off the lorry for three days. I thought they would be very stiff when they arrived at the trainer's stables near the racecourse in Madrid. However, they all came off bouncing with tails held high and executing high stepping trots, as if they were ready to go to the start of the Derby! One of them had exercised himself in his stall by kicking and diving backwards and forwards for want of something to do. None of them was unduly stressed but they did appreciate a good roll in deep straw when we led them into their boxes in the early hours of the morning.

However, travelling affects different horses in a variety of ways. Mental stress compounds physical exhaustion. If a horse is distressed, adrenalin is released into the bloodstream, which in the wild would either cause an aggressive or flight response, but all that it can do in the case of the horse being travelled is to increase its blood pressure, so if a horse is badly driven it will inevitably arrive at its destination in poor shape. A typical example are horses rammed into meat lorries which quickly become distressed and sustain injuries. It is a sad fact that the meat traders are allowed to get away with it on the basis that no one sees what happens in an enclosed lorry and as the horses are going to be killed anyway nobody bothers to take civilised precautions.

Travelling Abroad

If you venture abroad you will have to prepare yourself for endless official paperwork and health certificates, while in some cases blood tests will have to be made in advance. You will need advice from your vet and the Ministry of Agriculture on this, much depending on your destination.

On the ferry you will have to open vents, doors and windows and also lower the ramp if there is room to do so. If not, it can be partially wedged open by using a wooden block so that it cannot slam shut and by fixing ropes on the top to prevent it from dropping on a vehicle behind.

Remove the horse's top rug otherwise it will become far too hot, and ask the officer in charge of loading if it is possible to be parked under a fan. A little bicarbonate in the horse's feed will settle its stomach and encourage it to keep drinking. You will require some sort of manger which the animal cannot knock to the floor. Mangers are supplied with some makes of horsebox and fit into slots in front of the horse. If this facility is lacking tie up a bucket, but make sure that it is really firmly held.

Don't forget to take sufficient water-buckets with you on any journey and remember that you can reduce the amount of oats in the feed and substitute a higher percentage of dampened bran. The horse will be all the better for it, even if

Never leave chewable garments within range of a horse or pony

it is going to take part in a competition.

Lorry engines are not supposed to be left on in the hold of a ferry, but occasionally I have found that the engine of a refrigerated articulated vehicle has been left running. This must always be reported to the purser or officer in charge, otherwise a horse could be asphyxiated. Years ago this did, in fact, happen on a long sea crossing and seven show-jumpers were killed by poisonous fumes.

One minor hint, but one worth remembering wherever you are travelling, be it abroad or at home, is never to leave a jacket or any clothing in front of a horse where it can reach it. A friend left her daughter's best show jacket hanging over the breast-bar in a trailer, within reach of her pony. The latter chewed, dropped, pawed and finally staled on it – an expensive mistake!

.Chapter.
7

Horses, Travelling and the Law

7

Whether you purchase a new horsebox or trailer, obtain a second-hand one privately or from a dealer, or convert a horsebox yourself, it is essential, certainly for your own peace of mind, that you remain within the terms of the law considered from every angle. You must be totally conversant with speed limits, tachographs, payloads, who has permission to drive what in relation to weights and how you are not allowed to travel your horse or pony.

The maximum speed you are permitted to tow a trailer is 60mph (96km/ph). This relates to a passenger vehicle, motor-caravan, car-derived van or dual-purpose vehicle such as a Land-Rover. It does not, of course, mean that you have to travel at 60mph (96km/ph) for the sake of it, and indeed it is frequently unsafe so to do. Towing live animals in a trailer is very different from towing with a static load or pulling a caravan, so do use common sense.

If your towing vehicle comes within the above category the legal maximum weight it can tow is 3½ tons, on an over-run braking system, which is the standard system used on trailers. The trailer on its own must not weigh more than 1 ton unladen. You do not necessarily have to tow up to the maximum weight and you should take note of your recommended trailer weights.

Each manufacturer normally publishes a weight which accounts for the engine size of the car, the weight of the car, its length, gearing and suspension, all of which must be taken into account when towing. It is particularly important to take note of these factors when you decide upon the size of the trailer and the animals you will be carrying because you could lend yourself open to prosecution if it is considered that the load you are towing is unsafe. Most vehicles can set a trailer in motion but it takes an exceptional one to stop safely in an emergency.

One disadvantage of the higher speed limit is that some

drivers may ignore the feelings of the horse in the trailer and may be totally ignorant of the sensations created because, of course, it is illegal for humans to travel in moving trailers or caravans. Regulations differ slightly for drivers towing with a goods vehicle such as a motorised horsebox or van. To discover your speed limit you must add the manufacturer's gross weight of the box or van to the gross weight of the towing vehicle. This is the loaded weight which is usually inscribed on a plate on the vehicle. If this total does not exceed 7½ tons, your maximum speed is 60mph (96km/ph) on motorways and dual carriageways and 50mph (80km/ph) on all other roads. You must bear in mind, however, that if your gross weight does exceed 7½ tons in this category, whether towing or not, you will need to have a Heavy Goods Vehicle driver's licence. Your vehicle may be under the restricted weight on its own, but it may be over 7½ tons with a trailer. Your maximum speed in this case should be 60mph (96km/ph) on motorways, 50mph (80km/ph) on dual carriageways and 40mph (68km/ph) on all other roads.

If you intend to make a business out of your animals, and your goods carrying vehicle and trailer exceed 3½ tons gross weight when added together, you must have a tachograph fitted. Horseboxes up to 7½ tons gross vehicle weight may be driven by anyone who is 18 years of age or over, provided they have a car driving licence, while those below 3½ tons GVW may also be driven by 17-year-olds. The latter type of horsebox does not require a tachograph, log book or operator's licence when used professionally. This means that an owner may let it out for hire without breaking the law or having to undergo stringent tests now required before an operator's licence is granted.

In mid-1985 the Department of Transport announced that it intended to step up its campaign against overloaded lorries, and would employ more staff at roadside checks. This referred to all types of lorries, not just those carrying horses or other livestock. The number of weigh-bridges to check the weight of each axle was also to be increased.

A representative of the Department of Transport suggested that a statement of payload in advertisements selling horseboxes would be a help and a guidance for both the prospective purchaser and the driver. To avoid overloading a horsebox it is essential that the payload of the vehicle is known. This is the difference between the gross plated weight as it appears on the plating certificate and the weight of the box, including all partitions, rubber mats, etc, but excluding horses, humans, tack, feed and luggage. It is this figure which governs how great a load the lorry may carry and not the number of stalls fitted.

In extreme cases the Department of Transport can place a prohibition order on an overweight lorry, which means that the driver is not allowed to move it, but must obtain the assistance of another lorry to remove part of the load. Under these circumstances a commercial haulier could have his operator's licence withdrawn. However, it applies equally to private owners of horseboxes, so that the utmost care must be taken when checking payloads.

People still unwittingly advertise down-rated vehicles, designating them as original specification regarding the number of horses they can carry. This is not good news from the manufacturer's point of view.

A down-rated vehicle is one whose chassis was originally designed in excess of 7½ tons gross and therefore one requiring an HGV licensed driver. In the case of some lorries it is possible to carry out modifications which will reduce the gross plated weight and, in turn, the payload. This then brings it within the scope of a non-HGV licensed driver. It is these horseboxes which in their original specification state 'six horse box' but which, with their new reduced gross weight, may no longer be able to carry half-a-dozen full-sized horses.

It is the duty of owners to drive their vehicles over a weigh-bridge and carefully to calculate the weight of the horses and equipment and then to add the two results together. If the total exceeds the gross plated weight – and remember each axle is weighed separately – measures will have to be taken to keep within that weight, perhaps by reducing the weight of the vehicle in some way. If you are converting a lorry, you may find that the stalls are incorrectly partitioned for the stipulated axle weights.

Any horsebox is liable to a random check, from the smallest to the largest, and private vehicles are quite as likely to be scrutinised and weighed as are commercial ones. At the time of writing, the fines for driving an overweight lorry are a maximum of £2,000, although the level of fine is at the discretion of the individual magistrate. It is therefore in your own interest to be aware of the problem and to take action if your vehicle is overweight. Ironically, one unfortunate victim whose brand-new luxurious horsebox was found to be overweight belonged to a branch of the mounted police!

As far as speed is concerned, the maximum speed permitted for horseboxes is set by the total weight of the box and load, as explained earlier in this chapter.

While tachographs are not required for private purposes in Britain where horseboxes are concerned, they are obligatory abroad, so that if you intend to drive on the Continent a tachograph must be installed.

If you are converting an ordinary lorry for use as a horsebox, ensure that you have a door fitted in the back which you can use to enter the box from the outside so that, if you want to check your horses, you do not have the bother of lowering the ramp. As well as being of practical assistance it is also a legal requirement for safety reasons. Be certain, too, that you have sufficient ventilation. Alloy lorries can become exceedingly hot in warm weather and on several occasions I have seen small lorries at small class sales arrive with no ventilation – and in two cases with no ramp either.

You should note that it is illegal to travel horses loose if the sexes and sizes differ. It is only permissible in the case of such animals as youngsters from the New Forest sales which are used to being in a herd and which would panic if placed in stalls. It would be impossible to tie them up as they have rarely been handled or halter broken. However, you must not place a strong, stroppy colt in with fillies as he would only annoy them and spend the whole time chasing them around the box, causing unnecessary distress.

As I have said before, do not travel more than two horses loose if they are wearing shoes and do not mix very small animals, including foals, with larger horses. The small ones will eventually be kicked or bruised, or even break a leg.

It is worth noting that while commercial horse transporters' lorries are insured for carrying horses, each individual horse carried is not necessarily insured if it injures itself or dies. It is in your own interest to insure your own horses individually, otherwise you may find yourself involved in a loop-hole of the law which operates against you. I need hardly add that horseboxes must, by law, be insured and that trailers should also be covered.

Chapter 8

Rail, Sea and Air Transport

8

Where considerable distances are involved then rail, sea and air travel must be used. Transporting horses by rail is now rarely, if ever, undertaken in Britain as there are so many more horseboxes on the road today than thirty or forty years ago. In the latter part of the last century horses were regularly taken by rail for a day's hunting, special boxes being attached and shunted into sidings at the destination. Army horses used to travel by train, sometimes side-by-side in cattle-type wagons, or in partitioned stalls. I recall putting a show-jumper on a train from York to Hampshire in 1958. It had a very comfortable stall with ample bedding and a manger; there were three stalls at either end of the wagon facing each other. On the Continent, however, horses are still regularly travelled by train.

In the film *Lawrence of Arabia* there is a most interesting sequence depicting horses travelling in open wagons across the desert. The train was stopped, the sides of the wagons opened and the horses were shooed out. They all leapt down a considerable drop onto the sand, but landed safely. Army horses must have frequently been travelled in this manner, though how many came to harm is not recorded! Presumably they were watered from time to time otherwise they would have collapsed in the heat.

On the Continent excellent 'Fourgon' wagons are used to travel show-jumpers which have to be moved very long distances. They look much like passenger coaches externally, but the interior is divided into two looseboxes, one at either end, with space between for forage, trunks and other equipment. Horses competing at shows are more often than not returning to the point from which they set out, so the same wagons return, whereas horses being sold are usually placed in cattle-wagons.

I had the misfortune to travel in a cattle-wagon from Dunkirk to Rome one freezing January in 1976. One of the horses panicked as we started loading and the thought of spending two to three days in the wagon with it and three other horses, with no proper partitions to separate them, no lights or communication cord, was appalling. In the end I was joined by another assistant and the first night was spent trying to calm the panicking horse and the one next to it. After a sleepless night we got hold of a strong cattle gate and fixed it firmly in front of them with ropes so that they couldn't escape, and we could get some sleep. The troublemaker kicked all the way to Rome, the wagon was regularly shunted, we had no heat as we didn't dare light a stove for fear of fire and by the time we reached our destination I swore never again!

I recall travelling to the Rome International Show in a 'Fourgon' wagon from Boulogne in April 1978, having taken the horses across the Channel in a horsebox on the ferry. Horses and humans were most comfortable. The horses had straw to their bellies, and once they were used to the train they relaxed and laid down for part of the journey. The advantage of travelling like this is that the horses can rest

Three Arabs loaded into a pallet at Heathrow cargo

when they want, have room to move about and do not become too stiff. Sadly, all too many horses are even today travelled under appalling conditions when they are being sent for slaughter.

On much longer journeys, the chief problem is often one of overheating as the external temperature changes. In 1979 I travelled two horses and a pony by box to Greece. The horses were clipped and I was able to change their rugs as the hold became increasingly stuffy, but the pony had a thick woolly coat and sweated far more than was good for him. I now always advise owners to clip winter coats if the horses are travelling through changing temperatures. Rugs can always be taken off quickly, but the natural coat cannot.

A friend travelled with ten horses by sea to Australia in 1973 and found herself in trouble when a foal became overheated. She only managed to save it by keeping its ears cool with constantly renewed wet flannels.

Working out the amount of food required for a long journey is quite complex and I invariably advise taking more bedding and forage than you think you require. In 1986 some polo ponies were sent from Australia to England and ran out of food in the last week. They didn't look too well on arrival but survived with care.

Weather always affects horses on sea journeys, and Captains will usually refuse to take them if it is blowing over Force 7. Some horses travel as far as Australia by sea, although today most go by air. In the past they were travelled in wooden crates smaller than the average loosebox, and were swung onto the deck in a narrow crate by a crane. This could be alarming as a groom usually accompanied the horse and there was no way out if something went wrong! Now horses usually travel in well-designed crates winched on deck by massive machinery.

Many horses now travel by air. It is expensive but well justified in most cases, such as Thoroughbred mares being sent to an American stud or racehorses to contest a race. Many are flown to France instead of going by sea as they do not get travel-weary and keep their condition for the races.

Yearling trotters loaded in their pallet with plenty of hay

Pallets being loaded into the nose of a jumbo jet

Horses are usually loaded in pallets at the airport, often under cover of a shed. The horsebox ramp is dropped onto the ramp of the pallet, thereby preventing any awkward loaders escaping and galloping round the tarmac. This happened in 1974 when an American Quarterhorse went berserk in fog. New York airport had to be closed to all air traffic for three hours because the horse could neither be seen nor caught. The pallets are towed to the plane by airport tractors and are usually winched up in to it. Once in the plane, the pallets are pushed along on rollers and manoeuvred into position by handlers. A few planes still have the old-fashioned long ramp covered in straw up which the horses walk into the plane. The sides are high and covered in so that the animals cannot fall off.

If anything goes wrong in the air it could prove fatal, and a friend had a terrifying experience whilst flying two show-jumpers to Geneva. The plane hit turbulence over the Channel and one of the horses panicked and leapt forward over the door, suspending itself there on its belly. If it had gone right over it would probably have had to be shot. However the horse was calmed and held in that position for the remainder of the flight – over an hour. The co-pilot was very worried as the horse had reared and damaged some cables in the roof which affected the landing gear. By a miracle they made it, if a trifle bumpily, and all was well. Nowadays really strong, roomy and well designed pallets are used with a high door in front so that a horse cannot climb over.

When a plane takes off it can be alarming for a horse as it feels as if its hind legs are giving way. I stood in front of two horses on my first flight with ten to Copenhagen in 1970 and noticed my own legs felt weak, a new sensation as previously I'd always been sitting when taking off. The best thing to do is hold the horses' heads over the top of the door and pull them forward as the plane rises so that they don't sink down backwards, and then attempt to keep forwards to pull themselves up again. Most pilots are excellent if they know there are horses aboard and will not take off too steeply.

Horse pallets being loaded into a Flying Tigers jumbo at Heathrow

Landing is seldom too much of a problem; by then the horses have settled and don't realise what is happening until they are down. It is a good idea to have a haynet in front of them throughout the journey so they do not become bored.

It goes without saying that experienced handlers are necessary on flights. You can understand how dangerous it could be if a horse panicked on a plane and nobody knew what to do.

I hope I have covered all aspects of travel with horses by road, rail, sea and air, and that this book will be of help to those who read it. I wish you good, safe travelling, whatever mode of transport you wish to use.

Acknowledgements

The authors would like to thank Dr Sharon Cregier, Miss Sarah Jackson and Mr Bob Brastock for their help in preparing this book.

Index